THE HAMLYN LECTURES

TWENTY-EIGHTH SERIES

THE NATIONAL INSURANCE COMMISSIONERS

AUSTRALIA
The Law Book Company Ltd.
Sydney : Melbourne : Brisbane

CANADA AND U.S.A.
The Carswell Company Ltd.
Agincourt, Ontario

INDIA
N. M. Tripathi Private Ltd.
Bombay

ISRAEL
Steimatzky's Agency Ltd.
Jerusalem : Tel Aviv : Haifa

MALAYSIA : SINGAPORE : BRUNEI
Malayan Law Journal (Pte) Ltd.
Singapore

NEW ZEALAND
Sweet & Maxwell (N.Z.) Ltd.
Wellington

PAKISTAN
Pakistan Law House
Karachi

THE NATIONAL INSURANCE COMMISSIONERS

BY

SIR ROBERT MICKLETHWAIT,

Q.C., M.A., HON. LL.D.

formerly Chief National Insurance Commissioner

Published under the auspices of

THE HAMLYN TRUST

LONDON

STEVENS & SONS

1976

Published in 1976
by Stevens & Sons Limited
of 11 New Fetter Lane in
the City of London and
printed in Great Britain by
The Eastern Press Limited
of London and Reading

ISBN Hardback 0 420 45030 0
Paperback 0 420 45020 3

These lectures are dedicated
to the memory of
Archbishop William Temple,
who is thought to have been the first
to use in print the phrase
" The Welfare State." *

* See p. 6, n. 6.

CONTENTS

THE HAMLYN LECTURES

1949 Freedom under the Law
by The Rt. Hon. Lord Denning

1950 The Inheritance of the Common Law
by Richard O'Sullivan, Esq.

1951 The Rational Strength of English Law
by Professor F. H. Lawson

1952 English Law and the Moral Law
by Dr. A. L. Goodhart

1953 The Queen's Peace
by Sir Carleton Kemp Allen

1954 Executive Discretion and Judicial Control
by Professor C. J. Hamson

1955 The Proof of Guilt
by Dr. Glanville Williams

1956 Trial by Jury
by The Rt. Hon. Lord Devlin

1957 Protection from Power under English Law
by The Rt. Hon. Lord MacDermott

1958 The Sanctity of Contracts in English Law
by Sir David Hughes Parry

1959 Judge and Jurist in the Reign of Victoria
by C. H. S. Fifoot, Esq.

1960 The Common Law in India
by M. C. Setalvad, Esq.

1961 British Justice: The Scottish Contribution
by Professor T. B. Smith

1962 Lawyer and Litigant in England
by The Hon. Mr. Justice Megarry

1963 Crime and the Criminal Law
by The Baroness Wootton of Abinger

THE HAMLYN TRUST

THE Hamlyn Trust came into existence under the will of the late Miss Emma Warburton Hamlyn, of Torquay, who died in 1941 at the age of eighty. She came of an old and well-known Devon family. Her father, William Bussell Hamlyn, practised in Torquay as a solicitor for many years. She was a woman of strong character, intelligent and cultured, well versed in literature, music and art, and a lover of her country. She inherited a taste for law, and studied the subject. She also travelled frequently on the Continent and about the Mediterranean, and gathered impressions of comparative jurisprudence and ethnology.

Miss Hamlyn bequeathed the residue of her estate in terms which were thought vague. The matter was taken to the Chancery Division of the High Court, which on November 29, 1948, approved a Scheme for the administration of the Trust. Paragraph 3 of the Scheme is as follows:

> "The object of the charity is the furtherance by lectures or otherwise among the Common People of the United Kingdom of Great Britain and Northern Ireland of the knowledge of the Comparative Jurisprudence and the Ethnology of the chief European countries including the United Kingdom, and the circumstances of the growth of such jurisprudence to the intent that the Common People of the United Kingdom may realise the privileges which in law and custom they enjoy in comparison with other European Peoples and realising and appreciating such privileges may recognise the responsibilities and obligations attaching to them."

From the first the Trustees decided to organise courses of lectures of outstanding interest and quality by persons of eminence, under the auspices of co-operating Universities or other bodies, with a view to the lectures being made available in book form to a wide public.

The Twenty-Eighth Series of Hamlyn Lectures was delivered in May 1976 by Sir Robert Micklethwait at the New Senate Hall in Old College, Edinburgh University.

J. N. D. ANDERSON,
Chairman of the Trustees.

May 1976

ACKNOWLEDGMENTS

I am glad to have the opportunity of thanking those to whom I am indebted in connection with these lectures. They include the Hamlyn Trustees for doing me the honour of inviting me to give them; Edinburgh University and its Law Faculty for their hospitality in arranging for them to be delivered in the University; Lord Pearson and Sir David Renton for their ready agreement to my making use of materials submitted as written evidence to the Royal Commission and the Committee chaired by them; Lord Justice Scarman for kindly lending me notes of his Upjohn Lecture; Miss Florence Searls (formerly of the Commissioners' London office) for help in many ways; Mrs. Hilary Greenway for her admirable services as typist; and the publishers, whose great help included the preparation of the tables and index.

I am grateful too to many others, but for whom these lectures would never have been written: to all those with whom I have had over the years so many friendly and stimulating discussions on national insurance, and who have helped me in a variety of ways; to the Commissioners present and past; to many others who have worked in the Commissioners' offices; and to those in universities and elsewhere in this country and overseas who have shared my interest in the subject matter of the lectures and given me the benefit of their views.

In expressing the opinions that I have in the lectures I have spoken for myself alone, and not for the other Commissioners. The responsibility for any errors is my own.

After Chapter 10 had been sent to the printers the Law Commission's Report on Remedies in Administrative Law (Law. Com. No. 73) was published. Simplification of the legal machinery is of course always desirable, but apart from that I can see no need in the field which I discuss in these lectures for a remedy other than certiorari. The *Punton* case is commented on in the Report at pp. 13–14.

TABLE OF CASES

[For the significance of the titles of Commissioners' decisions see pp. 75–77, below. The presence of an asterisk (*) means that a judgment of a court is added as an appendix after the Commissioner's reported decision. I am authorised by the Chief Commissioner to say that where the shorthand note is the only record of a judgment, application may be made to the Commissioners' office for help. Where no page number appears opposite to a case, reference may be made to p. 124, below.]

PART 1

Commissioners' Decisions

PART 2

TABLE OF STATUTES

TABLE OF STATUTORY INSTRUMENTS

ABBREVIATIONS

A. A.	Attendance Allowance
A. A. Board	includes its delegate
App.	Appendix
benefits	the benefits now provided by the 1975 Act
Blue Book	"The I.I. Acts and regulations" (to 1975)
C.A.B.'s	Citizens' Advice Bureau(x)
the Consequential Provisions Act	The S.S. (Consequential Provisions) Act 1975
D.H.S.S. or the Department	The Department of Health and Social Security
D.C.Q.	Determination of Claims and Questions
F.A.N.I.	Family Allowances and National Insurance
Franks	The Report (Cmnd. 218) of the Committee on Administrative Tribunals and Enquiries
Industrial Injuries Acts or I.I. Acts	The National Insurance (Industrial Injuries) Acts
i.i. benefits	the benefits now provided by the 1975 Act, Part II, Chapter IV (formerly by the I.I. Acts)
IIAC	the Industrial Injuries Advisory Council
J	Dr. Jenkins' Index and Digest of Commissioners' Decisions (the Green Book)
L.A.G.	the Legal Action Group
n. (nn.)	note(s)
N.I.	National Insurance
n.i. benefits	the benefits now provided by the 1975 Act, Part II, Chapters I and II (formerly by the N.I. Acts)
NIAC	the National Insurance Advisory Committee
NILT	national insurance local tribunal
the 1946, 1965, 1970, etc. Acts	the National Insurance Acts, 1946, 1965, 1970, etc.
the 1973 and 1975 Acts	the Social Security Acts 1973 and 1975
P.D.	Prescribed Disease
para.	paragraph
Red Book	"The F.A. and N.I. Acts and regulations" (to 1975)
reg.(s)	regulation(s)
Renton	Report: The Preparation of Legislation (Cmnd. 6053)
S.I.	Statutory Instrument
S.S.	Social Security
s., ss.	section(s) (of the 1975 Act unless otherwise stated)
S.S. Act benefits	benefits (as above) (formerly provided by the N.I. and I.I. Acts)
Sched.	Schedule (to the 1975 Act unless otherwise stated)
the statutory authorities	the insurance officer, local tribunal and Commissioner (and see p. 18)
the user	see p. 80
U.S.I.	Unemployment, Sickness and Invalidity

CHAPTER ONE

INTRODUCTION

LADIES AND GENTLEMEN,

You would not, I suppose, wish me to occupy much of your time with expressions of gratitude and acknowledgements of help, but I cannot begin these lectures without at once expressing, however briefly, my deep gratitude to the Hamlyn Trustees for having invited me to deliver the lectures, and to the University of Edinburgh and the Faculty of Law for having invited me to deliver them here. I take this as a special compliment, since this University has played and is playing an important part in the field of law with which I shall be dealing, not only in participating in the important research into the activities of national insurance local tribunals conducted under the leadership of Professor Kathleen Bell of Newcastle upon Tyne University [1] and being one of those universities which include social security law in their syllabus, but also in pioneering the conferences of chairmen of such tribunals. The importance of the work of those tribunals has been long recognised, and for years it was being urged by the Council on Tribunals and others that conferences of their chairmen ought to be held periodically. It was Edinburgh University which arranged the first conference (including some tribunal members other than chairmen) and it was held in June 1972. This valuable initiative eventually led to conferences being held in other regions under the Lord Chancellor's auspices.[2] Having said this, I must immediately tender two apologies. First, to all Scotsmen. The statute law, both substantive and procedural, relating to national insurance and social security is, so far as relevant to these lectures, identical in England, Scotland and Wales, which together for these purposes form a single unit.[3] There will however inevitably be references to the law outside those statutes, and they I am afraid will necessarily be to the law of England, the only system in which I have had any training. Secondly, I must apologise to all Welshmen, since for brevity I refer to the law of England when I should perhaps in the spirit of the Welsh Language Act be referring to the law of England and Wales.[4]

The subject of these lectures is the National Insurance Commissioners. Each Commissioner individually is a statutory tribunal. Collectively they form the top tier of what I propose to call an "extended-three-tier-plus" adjudication structure for deciding claims for benefits under the Social Security Act 1975 and for family allowances.[5]

During the last two years most of the statutes and regulations governing this branch of the law have been repealed and replaced. Even before that, however, knowledge of it in the practising and academic legal profession was very uneven: some academic lawyers were familiar with much of it; most practising lawyers, except local and medical appeal tribunal chairmen, knew little of it and cared even less. This poses difficulties for a lecturer. Where a common foundation of learning cannot be assumed, it is all too easy to give lectures which will be uninteresting to those who are expert and unintelligible to those who are not. Further, the book which results from these lectures is expected to contain, as mine does, far more material than could be fitted into four lectures. I have therefore divided the book into chapters, some of which will form the lectures and some not. I have made extensive use of notes at the end of each chapter containing details which I hope will be helpful as signposts to beginners who wish to pursue their studies further in unfamiliar territory.

My approach to these lectures has been a purely personal one. Discussion of the Welfare State,[6] or social security (whatever that means), or even what has been called national insurance could range over a huge area and touch on many problems including political, social and economic ones. It could fill many books. The subject-matter of my lectures is much narrower. I shall not discuss such general questions as whether benefits and contributions in Great Britain should be more or less high or wide than they are, nor how our systems compare with those of other countries. I shall not even discuss the immensely important socially cohesive effects, both vertical and horizontal, of the national insurance and family allowance systems: vertical in that the more fortunate, whether they like it or not, provide help as contributors or taxpayers (or both) for those entitled to benefits or allowances (nobody can just " pass by on the other side "); and horizontal, in that for these purposes, as I have said, England, Scotland and Wales form one unit. I also think that it would be premature for me to discuss in these lectures the probable effects on this branch of the law, both substantive and procedural, of our membership of the European Economic Community.[7] My purpose is to discuss from personal experience the working of a particular system of legal adjudication, which in part was a novel experiment. For over 16 quite recent years, from the beginning of 1959 to my retirement in May 1975, I was myself a Commissioner. For the last 14 of those years I held the office now known as that of the Chief National Insurance Commissioner. During those years I noticed that many lawyers and others representing claimants had no idea of the special characteristics of the substantive law being administered; nor of the practice, procedure and rules of evidence, which they assumed would be the same as in the courts; nor of the spirit in which claims are judged by the statutory authorities, as the insurance officer, the local tribunal and the Commissioner are called. It was evident that a special combination of formality and informality was needed if one was to give an adequate hearing to the average claimant who was unrepresented, especially if he was also uneducated or even illiterate. Finally, I was able to see something of the processes by which the law is made, in statutes and regulations, by the courts and the Commissioners, and the help given by local tribunals in these processes. I noted areas where I thought that the law and some of the law-making processes could be improved, and formed opinions as to the means by which I think they should be.

With these matters in mind I decided that the best contribution that I could make towards increasing the learning about the work of the Commissioners was to make available to all who might be interested the fruits of my own practical experience as a Commissioner, by recording matters of fact and procedure not discoverable by the practitioner easily, if at all, from books, and making some suggestions as to how the law might be improved.

My main purposes therefore are as follows. I have tried to describe the, partly experimental, system of legal adjudication in which the Commissioners play a part; to draw attention to some of the special characteristics of the branches of the law with which they are concerned; to explain the manner in which they administer it, openly, independently and in accordance with the rules laid down in the legislation and case law; and to indicate the spirit in which it is administered at every level. I have gone on to suggest, in some detail, ways in which the substantive law in this field could be improved, not by changing its objectives, which are political matters, but by making it say more clearly and simply what it is trying to say, and to suggest a way in which the machinery for improving it could and should be further developed. I hope that by the end of the lectures I shall have persuaded you that I am right in believing, as I most profoundly do, that the "extended-three-tier-plus" adjudication structure is a most excellent one, admirably suited to its purpose, and it should on no account be replaced by a two-tier one, as has been suggested.

Finally I hope that at least some more members of the legal profession will come to see that there is a real need for the profession to play a far greater part than it does in national insurance work, in the interests of the public as well as its own.

Some lawyers may say: "Why should we interest ourselves in this branch of the law? It seems to have managed without us up to now. Anyway there is no money in it." In reply I will for the moment say merely this. The law administered by the Commissioners affects or will affect practically everyone in Britain. Its influence is vast. Every year some 15 to 20 million claims for benefit are decided by insurance officers, from whose decisions there are some 30,000 appeals to local tribunals and some 2,000 further appeals to Commissioners.[8] The total amount of benefit paid out yearly had by December 1975 risen to over 8,500 million pounds.[9] Contrary to the belief of many lawyers an award, particularly of industrial disablement benefit, can be substantial. Such an award consists of weekly payments, tax free, " indexed " so that the weekly rate is increased even in respect of past awards as the cost of living goes up. For a very grave industrial accident an award could be equivalent to well over £4,000 yearly, tax free and indexed; and the value of this indexing can be judged from the fact that one element worth the equivalent of £2·25 weekly in 1951 had by December 1975 become £21·80 weekly.[10] If one tries to capitalise the value of such an award, assuming that it will continue to be paid for life, taking into account tax and present and future inflation, one cannot say with confidence that its value is necessarily less than some of the bigger awards made in the High Court. It cannot be right from the public point of view that claimants for substantial sums should not be legally represented simply because most of the legal profession are not interested. From the legal profession's point of view, the Bar's former monopoly of representative advocacy in the courts has to a considerable extent been eroded in favour of others. The regulations governing appeals to the statutory authorities expressly enable any person entitled to be heard to be represented by anyone.[11] Claimants are already to an appreciable extent being represented by persons without professional legal qualifications. The longer and the more extensively that this goes on the more likely it would be to constitute a threat to the interests of the legal profession. Lord Justice Scarman made this point powerfully in his Upjohn Lecture [12] and elsewhere, and I respectfully agree with him.[13]

Notes

1 See the *Journal of Social Policy,* Vol. 3, Pt. 4, pp. 289–315 and Vol. 4, Pt. 1, pp. 1–24. See also p. 67, n. 7, below.

2 See the Reports of the Council on Tribunals 1969–70, para. 27, 1970–71, para. 21, and 1971–72, para. 23, and p. 146, n. 54, below.

3 Statutes which apply in Scotland as well as England are usually administered in England by English courts or tribunals and in Scotland by Scottish ones. There are comparatively few legal procedures in respect of which England and Scotland are one unit. National insurance procedure is one of them. Like a local tribunal, a Commissioner whether he works in England, Scotland or Wales has jurisdiction to decide

appeals coming from any of the three countries, irrespective of the question in which of them the claim originated or in which of them the decision of the tribunal, from which the appeal comes, was given. This single, undivided jurisdiction has great advantages which will be noticed later. (See p. 48.)

[4] The Welsh Language Act 1967, s. 4, which deleted the words " dominion of Wales " from an earlier statute.

[5] Governed by the Family Allowances Act 1965, until it is replaced by child benefit under the Child Benefit Act 1975.

[6] The phrase " the Welfare State " was used by Archbishop Temple in his pamphlet " Citizen and Churchman " (1941) at p. 35, where he wrote: " In place of the conception of the Power-State we are led to that of the Welfare-State." It has been said that this probably was the first use of the phrase in print; see J. F. Sleeman, *The Welfare State* (1973) at p. 1, citing P. Gregg, *The Welfare State* (1967) at pp. 3–4.

[7] Decisions have already been given by a Commissioner on the meaning of some of the EEC regulations; see, *e.g.*, Decisions C.S. 4/74, C.I. 18/74, C.S. 1/75, C.F. 1/75, C.A. 3/75 and C.S.S. 2/75 (none yet reported). I understand that a reference by a Commissioner is pending on the application of the Secretary of the State to the European Court of Justice of questions arising in the above Decision C.S.S. 2/75 on the claim of a Mr. R. J. Brack (European Court Case No. 17/76).

[8] See the D.H.S.S. Annual Report 1974, Cmnd. 6150, Chap. 10. The figures for the Commissioners include applications and appeals coming from medical appeal tribunals and the Attendance Allowance Board.

[9] Information supplied by the Department.

[10] Basic disablement pension for 100 per cent. disability with maximum increases. For 1951, see the Tables of Main Rates, the Blue Book, p. 602; for 1975, the 1975 Act, Sched. 4, Pt. V, para. 3, as substituted by the Social Security Benefits Up-rating Order [1975] [S.I. 1975 No. 1096]. I have assumed the man to be young, married, with two children.

[11] See the S.S. (D.C.Q.) regs. 1975 [S.I. 1975 No. 558], reg. 3 (1) (*b*).

[12] See pp. 138–139, below.

[13] Lawyers wanting a bird's-eye view of national insurance benefits (after the 1975 Act) and many other forms of benefits and assistance may find helpful Smith and Hoath, *Law and the Underprivileged* (1975).

Chapter Two

CONSTRUCTION

To understand the work and the decisions of the Commissioners it is helpful to recall the stages by which their jurisdiction was built up.

The National Insurance Act 1946 and the National Insurance (Industrial Injuries) Act 1946 were two of the great statutes which following the Beveridge Report formed the foundation of what has now come to be called the Welfare State. They both came into effective operation on " the appointed day," July 5, 1948.[1]

The National Insurance Act 1946 took a number of legal rights arising out of such events as unemployment, sickness, old age, etc., which rights had been built up under earlier legislation, expanded and improved them and welded them into a universal, compulsory, mainly contributory state system of national insurance benefits. These benefits together with some others added later are fully discussed by Professor Harry Calvert in his book *Social Security Law*.[2] (From now on for brevity I will refer to this Act and the 1965 Act of the same name simply as " the 1946 and 1965 Acts.")

For present purposes it will suffice merely to list the benefits provided by the 1946 Act: unemployment benefit, sickness benefit, maternity benefit, widow's benefit, guardian's allowance, retirement pension and death grant.

Before the 1946 Act there had been a number of different systems of adjudication in this field. One, which had been outstandingly successful, had been built up since the introduction of unemployment benefit by the National Insurance Act 1911. It had provided for adjudication on claims for unemployment benefit by insurance officers, courts of referees, and the Umpire.[3]

The adjudication system introduced by the 1946 Act was different from any administered by the courts. It was clearly modelled on the earlier unemployment benefit system, but was now applied to all benefits. It distributed the duty of deciding various questions between various adjudicating authorities. Certain questions relating mainly to contributions and classification were entrusted to the Minister of National Insurance. Certain questions relating to children might be decided under the family allowance procedure, to which I shall refer later. All claims and all questions not entrusted to another adjudicating authority were for decision by the insurance officer, the local tribunal or the National Insurance Commissioner who collectively came to be known as they still are as " the statutory authorities." [4] The benefits provided by the 1946 Act were referred to as national insurance benefits, which enabled them to be readily distinguished from other benefits under other systems.

The National Insurance (Industrial Injuries) Act 1946 was designed to substitute for the provisions previously contained in the Workmen's Compensation Acts [5] a state system similar to the National Insurance system and forming with it and other legislation one composite whole. (From now on for brevity I will refer to this Act and to the 1965 Act of the same name simply as " the Industrial Injuries Acts.")

The nature of the benefits provided and the procedure relating to them under the Industrial Injuries Act are described in the speeches of the Lords of Appeal in the *Hudson* and *Jones* cases. The Act primarily provided benefits for personal injury by accident arising out of and in the course of the employment, but it was extended to cover certain prescribed diseases.[6]

This legislation has always provided three basic benefits for such accidents and prescribed diseases: (industrial) injury benefit during incapacity for work during a period not exceeding approximately six months after the accident; (industrial) disablement benefit, for, broadly speaking, any period after the injury benefit period; and (industrial) death benefit.[7]

Under this Act also the duty of deciding questions was distributed among different adjudicating authorities. The decision on any claim or question not entrusted for decision to others was here also entrusted to the insurance officer, the local appeal tribunal (not the local tribunal) and the Industrial Injuries Commissioner (not the National Insurance Commissioner) or one of the Deputy Commissioners. These three tiers of adjudicating authorities also came to be referred to as "the statutory authorities." Certain questions were to be decided by the Minister of National Insurance. These included exceptionally questions as to title (*i.e.* in effect claims) to the increase of industrial disablement benefit known as a constant attendance allowance and now also to the increase for exceptionally severe disablement.[8] Also some questions relating to children were decided under the Family Allowances Act procedure in much the same way as similar national insurance questions.

There were, however, other very important divisions of the jurisdiction. The Industrial Injuries Act 1946 provided for the setting up of certain medical authorities whose duties included not merely advising on medical questions but deciding them. These were medical boards consisting of two doctors,[9] whose decision might be referred on appeal or otherwise to a medical appeal tribunal. The Act provided that any decision of questions given in accordance with its provisions was final, and this coupled with the distribution of duties between the statutory and medical authorities has caused difficulty and controversy to which I shall have to refer briefly later.

The Industrial Injuries Act contained within it some seeds of confusion, but fortunately they were never allowed to grow. The short title of that Act contained the words "national insurance," so in a broad sense benefits under it could have been described as national insurance benefits. In practice, however, that phrase was limited to benefits under the National Insurance Act 1946,[10] and for all the benefits under the Industrial Injuries Act the generic term "industrial injuries (or injury) benefits" was used, and the similarity of that term to the specific term "industrial injury benefit," the full title of one of the three benefits under the Industrial Injuries Act 1946, or "injury benefit"[10] was never allowed to cause confusion.

The two 1946 Acts in effect constructed adjudication systems like two semi-detached three-storey houses, the two structures each containing three layers of statutory authorities who, though technically separate and called by different names, were very close neighbours. In fact at all times the National Insurance Commissioner and the Industrial Injuries Commissioner were one and the same person; and each Deputy Commissioner held appointments under both Acts. The titles of the Deputy Commissioners were somewhat cumbersome and not easy to abbreviate.

There were of course other parts of the whole social welfare system operating alongside the statutory authorities system and independently of it. One related to national assistance under the National Assistance Act 1948 and subsequent legislation which has amended or replaced it. The statutory authorities have never had jurisdiction in those fields.[11] Certain other duties of minor importance were entrusted then and since to the statutory authorities, but they raise no questions deserving discussion.[12] Another system operating alongside concerned family allowances but they did not come into the story until later.

In July 1957 the Committee on Administrative Tribunals and Enquiries, commonly known as the Franks Committee, published its report.[13] A number of events affecting the Commissioners resulted from the Committee's recommendations. The Tribunals and Inquiries Act 1958 created the Council on Tribunals, whom the Act charged with the duty of keeping under review the constitution and working of certain tribunals.[14] The Act made it clear that the Commissioner and each Deputy Commissioner under each of the systems individually constituted such a tribunal.[15] Another change directly resulting from a recommendation of the Committee had the effect that, though until then leave to appeal to the Commissioner had been necessary in some cases, from then onwards it was not necessary in any.[16] I have no doubt that this change was a wise one. It is true that as a result of it a certain number of frivolous or hopeless appeals come before the Commissioners. These, however, are not the appeals which occupy much time. Moreover granting leave to appeal and then, if leave is granted, later dealing with the appeal involves considering the case twice. From time to time it has been suggested that to reduce the Commissioners' work-load, a requirement of leave in some cases should be reintroduced, but I have yet to hear of any satisfactory dividing line, based on either the amount at stake or the type of proceeding or some other criterion, for deciding in which cases leave should be required.

The Commissioners' procedure was always governed by regulations.[17] Following recommendations of the Franks Committee the regulations were amended in 1958 in relation to the holding of hearings in public [18] and the calling of witnesses.[19] I have always understood that these changes had little practical effect, since the Commissioners were already following the procedures recommended.

An important change which resulted from a recommendation [20] of the Franks Committee was that the Family Allowances and National Insurance Act 1959, s. 1, transferred to the statutory authorities the duty of deciding claims for family allowances. Family allowances had first been introduced by the Family Allowances Act 1945. In 1945 the statutory authority system had not yet been set up, and claims for family allowances had been decided by the Minister, with a right of appeal to a family allowance referee.[21] This change went somewhat further than the Franks recommendation, in that it took away the duty of deciding the claim in the first instance from the Minister and handed it over to the insurance officer.

Section 2 of the 1959 Act effected an even more important change. It created for the first time a right of appeal from a medical appeal tribunal to the Industrial Injuries Commissioner, but only with leave and only on a question of law. This was a real innovation and experiment. Parliament was entrusting to one " inferior tribunal " the duty of correcting errors of law made by another such tribunal, without prejudice to the power of further correction by the courts. Appeals under this important new procedure came from the medical appeal tribunal direct to the Commissioner and not through the insurance officer or the local appeal tribunal. It left the three-tier system intact but added an extension of the Commissioner's jurisdiction. Some of the background to this change was briefly as follows. Medical appeal tribunals sat throughout Great Britain and each was presided over by one of about a dozen chairmen. They had to interpret and apply some complicated statutory provisions. There was no series of reports in which their more important decisions were circulated for the information of others. The result inevitably was that there was considerable inconsistency between the decisions of different tribunals in similar cases. One of the effects of section 36 of the Industrial Injuries Act 1946 was that a decision of a medical appeal tribunal was declared by statute to be "final." At first it was thought that therefore a decision of such a tribunal could not be challenged in the courts by any means. By 1957 at latest however, it had been clearly established that this view was wrong. In *Gilmore's* case a decision of a medical appeal tribunal was quashed by an order of certiorari. This case and others which followed it made it evident that there were going to be a number of similar cases coming before the High Court.[22]

I think that in the light of these decisions the creation of a right of appeal from a medical appeal tribunal to the Commissioner was an admirable method of dealing with the situation.

In 1958 proceedings were taken successfully in the *Hurst* case to quash a decision of the Commissioner on appeal from a local tribunal. The first attempt to do this had been in the *Timmis, Cox* and *James* cases in 1955, but this had failed on the facts. Further attempts were made in the *Richardson* case, unsuccessfully, and in the *Jones* (1962) case, successfully. By then it was clearly established that a Commissioner's decision under either of the 1946 Acts could be quashed by an order of certiorari for error in law. It is this addition to the three-tier structure that I have ventured to call the "plus."

Neither the consolidation of the three Acts by the National Insurance Act 1965, the National Insurance (Industrial Injuries) Act 1965 and the Family Allowances Act 1965 nor the amendments of the substantive law which took place in connection with it had much practical effect on the procedure of the Commissioners.

The next event of outstanding procedural importance was the

enactment of the National Insurance Act 1966. This made three material changes. A substantial change was that to a considerable extent it merged the adjudication procedure for industrial injury cases into the national insurance procedure.[23] From then onwards industrial injury claims were decided by the (renamed) national insurance statutory authorities: till then the insurance officer, the local tribunal (not the local appeal tribunal) and the National Insurance Commissioner (not the Industrial Injuries Commissioner) or one of the Deputy Commissioners. I have no doubt that this change was most beneficial. There had been a number of minor differences between the two procedures, which had acted merely as traps. The use of the national insurance procedure, with only stated modifications for industrial injury cases,[24] was far less likely to lead to error.

Secondly the 1966 Act altered the names of the offices of the National Insurance Commissioner and the Deputy Commissioners. These titles had for a long time caused inconvenience. The phrase National Insurance Deputy Commissioner was long and had never caught on. The formal name " Deputy Commissioner for the purposes of the National Insurance Acts " was worse. The names had caused misunderstanding in the minds of a substantial number of claimants, who could not believe that a decision given by a deputy was the real thing. Accordingly in place of the existing power to appoint the National Insurance Commissioner and Deputy Commissioners there was substituted a power to appoint a Chief National Insurance Commissioner (" the Chief Commissioner ") and other National Insurance Commissioners, and those already holding the former offices were deemed to have been appointed to the corresponding new offices.[25] The 1966 Act made no provision changing the name of the office of the Industrial Injuries Commissioner or his deputies. There was no need for it to do so. As a result of the first change effected by the Act we no longer had any duties in those capacities, though so far as I know our offices were not actually abolished.

The third change consisted of the introduction of another increase of disablement benefit in cases of exceptionally severe disablement. Claims for this increase were to be determined by the Minister (as they now are by the Secretary of State), just as claims for a constant attendance allowance always had been.[26]

In passing we should note that it was in 1966 that the Ministry of Social Security Act 1966 not only changed the name of the ministry but also set up the Supplementary Benefits Commission and substituted supplementary benefit for national assistance. The Commissioners, however, continued to have no jurisdiction to decide claims for supplementary benefit.[27]

Down to this point there was no substantial confusion as to terminology. Benefits provided by the three 1965 Acts were clearly distinguishable from each other by the names of the Acts governing them: national insurance benefits, industrial injuries (or injury) benefits and family allowances. They were equally distinguishable from supplementary benefit. It was later that unfortunately confusion as to the terminology crept in.

At the end of 1969 Mr. Richard Crossman who was then Secretary of State for Social Services introduced his National Superannuation and Social Insurance Bill. This Bill if enacted would have made important changes in the statutory authority procedure, but owing to the result of the 1970 General Election it was never enacted.

The National Insurance (Old Persons' and Widows' Pensions and Attendance Allowance) Act 1970 introduced attendance allowances on much the same lines as had been proposed in clause 17 of Mr. Crossman's Bill.[28] This new allowance was described in the 1970 Act as "an additional description of benefit under the principal Act," which was the 1965 Act. It followed that it was, as it still is, for the statutory authorities to decide both claims for the benefit and any questions, the decision of which was not entrusted to others. It was a non-contributory benefit and therefore no contribution questions arose for decision by the Secretary of State. Section 4 (2) of the Act, however, contained conditions of title to the benefit involving medical questions, and the duty of deciding whether those conditions were fulfilled was entrusted to the Attendance

Allowance Board set up under the 1970 Act,[29] who had power to delegate any of their functions in respect of an individual case to one or more medical practitioners.[30] This power was freely exercised. The medical practitioner is in practice referred to as a delegate. After a decision had been given by the board or a delegate there was a power within limits to review the decision.[31] This Act contained features which were novel in national insurance as opposed to industrial injury law. Questions arising on claims for some benefits such as sickness benefit raised medical questions, but these had always been decided by the statutory authorities. Now the decision of questions which contained a considerable element of medicine was being entrusted to others. Perhaps the nearest comparison is with the procedure on a claim for industrial disablement benefit or on a claim for injury benefit based on a prescribed disease, where certain medical questions are decided by doctors. The Act required regulations to enable appeals to be brought from a review decision to a National Insurance Commissioner with the leave of a Commissioner on a question of law arising on the review.[32] This again was an innovation and experiment similar to the one relating to medical appeal tribunals, the success of which doubtless encouraged the introduction of this one. This was a second " extension " of the jurisdiction of the Commissioners.

The 1970 Act and the National Insurance Act 1971 introduced further benefits, notably non-contributory benefits for persons who had attained certain advanced ages and invalidity benefit. These however were straightforward national insurance benefits, which created no new procedural problems affecting a Commissioner's jurisdiction.

We have now reached the early 1970s, where it may be convenient to pause and survey the position. The jurisdiction of the Commissioners had been built up substantially as it is now, the much later addition to it resulting from the introduction of the mobility allowance constituting an addition which will not materially affect its shape. Briefly summarised, the build-up has been as follows.

The Commissioners' jurisdiction on appeals from local

tribunals has existed in national insurance cases since 1948, in family allowance cases since 1959, and in industrial injury cases since 1966, when there was transferred to the National Insurance Commissioners the jurisdiction exercised by themselves since 1948 in a different capacity as the Industrial Injuries Commissioner and the Deputy Industrial Injuries Commissioners. The powers of a Commissioner on such appeals are extensive. His duty is to reconsider and decide all questions of fact as well as law. The proceedings are therefore, whether an oral hearing is held or not, a " rehearing " in the fullest sense of that term.

There has also been a right of appeal to a Commissioner with leave, on questions of law only, from a medical appeal tribunal in industrial injuries cases since 1959, and from the Attendance Allowance Board since 1970. Here the powers of the Commissioner are strictly limited. He has no power to substitute his own findings of fact for those of the tribunal or board. It will be noticed that the insurance officer and the local tribunal do not come into these last proceedings at all. These jurisdictions therefore form extensions of the Commissioners' jurisdiction rather than alterations to the three-tier structure.

The developments arising out of the introduction of the mobility allowance by the Social Security Pensions Act 1975 must be considered out of their chronological order. It is a new non-contributory benefit under the 1975 Act. The procedure for determining claims for this benefit and questions arising on such claims is an interesting variant of the industrial injuries procedure as modified for the purposes of prescribed disease cases.[33] It is for the statutory authorities to determine the claim for a mobility allowance and some questions; and on that part of the case there is an appeal on fact as well as law from the local tribunal to a Commissioner. Certain medical questions (as defined), however, are for decision by a medical board and medical appeal tribunal, with a right of appeal from the medical appeal tribunal to a Commissioner on a question of law only. This therefore is a further extension into the field of the medical appeal tribunal.[34]

In England a decision of a Commissioner in any of the above cases can be reviewed by the court, and there can be an appeal from the Divisional Court to the Court of Appeal and thence to the House of Lords.[35] These proceedings in the courts, however, are for a " prerogative " order (in practice certiorari) and technically do not constitute appeals. Hence my use of the word " plus " rather than describing the set-up as a six-tier adjudication structure. I have therefore coined the phrase " extended three-tier-plus " structure since it describes precisely what it is: the three tiers consist of the insurance officer, the local tribunal and the Commissioner; there are extensions into the areas of the medical appeal tribunal and the Attendance Allowance Board; and the " plus " represents the control of the Commissioners by the courts.

Another recent introduction is child interim benefit under Part II of the Child Benefit Act 1975, but the determination of questions under that Act is not entrusted to the statutory authorities.[36] The same Act enables regulations to vary the statutory authority procedure on the determination of claims for child benefit when it replaces family allowances, as is already the case on claims for family allowances.[37]

I think that down to about 1971 there was no serious ambiguity about the meaning of the various words used to describe benefits. My impression however is that in common parlance the phrase " social security " had come increasingly to mean or at least include supplementary benefit. If a woman told you that she was " on the Social Security," that was probably the benefit which she was drawing. It was after this time that the real confusion about words became serious, and the next chapter is devoted to that topic.

Notes

[1] Much of the credit for bringing this substantial body of legislation into force on the same day must go to the Rt. Hon. James Griffiths M.P. who was Minister of National Insurance from 1945 to 1950 and lived until 1975 to see that later alterations to the system were no more than additions built on the solid foundations which he had been largely instrumental in laying down.

[2] (1974) Published by Sweet and Maxwell, 11 New Fetter Lane, London. See also p. 6, n. 13.

[3] Selections of the Umpire's decisions were printed and published by H.M. Stationery Office and throw valuable light on many of the same problems with which the Commissioners are today confronted. A good description of the pre-1948 systems is contained in *Halsbury's Laws of England* (2nd (Hailsham), ed., 1940), Vol. 34, title "Work and Labour," which was contributed by Mr. Richard Ludlow, a barrister of great experience in this field who himself held office as deputy umpire from 1928 to 1947 and was knighted for his services in 1950.

[4] I have not been able to discover the origin of the phrase "the statutory authorities." I cannot remember having seen it in any National Insurance Act or regulation nor in earlier textbooks such as Potter and Stansfeld, *National Insurance* (2nd ed., 1949), see the notes to section 43. From an early stage, however, the phrase was habitually used by the Commissioners and others administering the Act. It appears in the introductory note to each of the first bound volumes of *Commissioner's Decisions* published in 1955 and in *Halsbury's Laws of England* (3rd (Simonds) ed., 1959), Vol. 27, title "National Insurance," p. 768. The phrase is now commonly used by everyone concerned with this branch of the law. Its first statutory appearance, however, so far as I have observed, is unexpectedly in s. 20 of the 1975 Act which deals with disqualification for misconduct, etc. S. 20 provides for disqualification for a period "determined in accordance with ss. 97–104 of the Act (adjudication by insurance officers and other statutory authorities . . .)." The phrase, however, does not appear in any of the latter sections. Nor is it defined in Sched. 20. In view of its common use I think this is unfortunate, since some claimants and other "users" (see p. 80) do not understand what it means. See also p. 45, n. 15.

[5] The background against which this 1946 Act was introduced is explained in Potter and Stansfeld, *National Insurance* (*Industrial Injuries*) (2nd ed., 1950), pp. 3–12. A much briefer description of some of the reasons for the change is contained in a lecture which I delivered to a number of learned bodies, one version of which is recorded in the *Medico-Legal Journal* (1969), Vol. 37, Pt. 4, p. 172.

[6] See Pt. IV of the Act and the N.I. (I.I.) (P.D.) regs. 1948 [S.I. 1948 No. 1371], now replaced by the S.S. (I.I.) (P.D.) regs. 1975 [S.I. 1975 No. 1537].

[7] See the I.I. Acts 1946, s. 7 and 1965, s. 5 and the 1975 Act, s. 50.

[8] See the I.I. Act 1946, ss. 15 and 36 (1) (*a*), the N.I. Act 1966, s. 6 and now the 1975 Act, ss. 61, 63 and 95 (1). As to the procedure by which such questions are determined and the manner in which the sections are interpreted the public can have no knowledge. There are no statutory rules governing the procedure, and I am not aware that any decisions have been published. For a strong criticism of the procedure

see David Carson, "National Insurance Law, Some More Secrecy" (1976) 126 N.L.J. 59.

[9] Or exceptionally one (ss. 38–41 of the Act).

[10] See p. 8, above.

[11] There was a tenuous link in that questions arising under s. 10 (relating to trade disputes) of the Ministry of Social Security Act 1966 (alias the Supplementary Benefit Act 1966) were to be decided by a local tribunal under the National Insurance Act, from whom an appeal lay to the Commissioner (see the 1966 Act, ss. 10 and 18 (2), replacing the National Assistance Act 1948, ss. 9 (3) and 14 (3)). Decisions under these sections form only a minute part of the work of the Commissioners. The only provision which did show signs of being controversial was the power of abatement contained in s. 16 (1A) of the Supplementary Benefit Act 1966 (as amended). This provides that "the relevant social security benefit may, at the discretion of the authority administering it, be abated . . ." by an amount determined by the Supplementary Benefits Commission. The question who is "the authority administering it" may be open to argument; see Decision C.P. 3/75 (not reported), paras. 19–24.

[12] See the Industrial Injuries and Diseases (Old Cases) Act 1975, s. 8 (3) (*b*) and the provisions relating to post-war credits and to payments of £10 to certain persons at Christmas 1972–74.

[13] Cmnd. 218. One member of the committee was Mr. Roderic Bowen Q.C. who is now the National Insurance Commissioner working in Cardiff.

[14] The 1958 Act, s. 1; now the Tribunals and Inquiries Act 1971, s. 1.

[15] S. 14 (2) and the First Sched., paras. 11 and 12, now replaced by the Tribunals and Inquiries Act 1971, s. 19 (3) and Sched. 1, Pt. I, para. 18. Whether those who criticise the work of social security tribunals in general terms are aware that their comments should properly be understood as referring to the Commissioners amongst others seems doubtful.

[16] *Franks*, Chap. 14 and para. 409 (46) and the F.A.N.I. Act 1959, s. 3.

[17] Originally the N.I. (D.C.Q.) regs. 1948 [S.I. 1948 No. 1144] and the N.I. (I.I.) (D.C.Q.) regs. 1948 [S.I. 1948 No. 1299], as amended.

[18] *Franks*, para. 81 and the N.I. (D.C.Q.) regs. 1958 [S.I. 1958 No. 701], reg. 4 (2). In industrial injury cases the hearing already had normally to be in public; see the N.I. (I.I.) (D.C.Q.) regs. 1948 [S.I. 1948 No. 1299], reg. 22 (3).

[19] *Franks*, para. 93, the N.I. (D.C.Q.) regs. 1958 [S.I. 1958 No. 701], reg. 4 (3) and N.I. (I.I.) (D.C.Q.) regs. 1958 [S.I. 1958 No. 702], reg. 2 (4).

[20] *Franks*, paras. 170, 184 and 409 (49).

[21] Selections of the decisions of the referees in such cases were circulated, and some of them form valuable additions to the thinking on the problems with which the Commissioners had later to deal. There

was no legal requirement that the Commissioner or any of the Deputy Commissioners should also be a referee, but in fact Sir Archibald Safford was.

[22] *e.g.*, the *Burpitt* case.

[23] S. 8.

[24] The 1966 Act, Sched. 2, and the N.I. (I.I.) (D.C.Q.) (No. 2) regs. 1967 [S.I. 1967 No. 1571], Sched. 1.

[25] See the N.I. Act 1966, s. 9.

[26] See the N.I. Act 1966, s. 6; now the 1975 Act, ss. 63 and 95.

[27] See, however, p. 10 and n. 11 on p. 19, above. For the change of name of the M.S.S. Act 1966 for certain purposes see below, p. 28.

[28] The 1970 Act, ss. 4 (1) and 8 (1). The effect of the N.I. Act 1972, s. 8 (4) as amended by the N.I. Act 1974, Sched. 4, para. 18 is that the 1970 Act may be cited as the National Insurance Act 1970 in any other Act, instrument or document, as it is in the 1972 Act.

[29] See the 1970 Act, ss. 5 (1) and 6 (2). The conditions were replaced by different ones contained in the N.I. Act 1972, s. 2, to enable the allowance to be paid at two different rates, but this change did not alter the procedure materially.

[30] See the 1970 Act, s. 5 (6); now the 1975 Act, Sched. 11, Pt. I, para. 5.

[31] See the 1970 Act, s. 6.

[32] See the 1970 Act, s. 6 (4) and the N.I. (A.A.) regs. 1971 [S.I. 1971 No. 621], Pt. VII; now the 1975 Act, ss. 35 and 106 (2) and the S.S. (A.A.) regs. 1975 [S.I. 1975 No. 496], Pt.VI.

[33] The mobility allowance was introduced by the S.S. Pensions Act 1975, s. 22, which inserted into the 1975 Act a new s. 37A. It is being made available to different age groups by stages; see the S.S. Pensions Act 1975 (Commencement No. 2) Order 1975 [S.I. 1975 No. 1572 (C. 45)] and the S.S. Pensions Act 1975 (Commencement No. 4) Order 1975 [S.I. 1975 No. 2079 (C. 58)]. The decision of certain medical questions by the medical board and medical appeal tribunal is provided for by the Mobility Allowance regs. 1975 [S.I. 1975 No. 1573], Pt. IV, which applies the 1975 Act, s. 112 (see reg. 19) with a minor modification.

[34] As to prescribed diseases, see the S.S. (I.I.) (P.D.) regs. 1975 [S.I. 1975 No. 1537], especially Pt. V.

[35] As to Scotland, see p. 124.

[36] See the Child Benefit Act 1975, s. 16 (7). Mr. Temple and Mr. Shewan (see p. 44, n. 8) have however been appointed to be Referees under s. 16 and the Child Interim Benefit (D.Q.) regs. 1975 [S.I. 1975 No. 1925].

[37] See the F.A. (D.C.Q.) (No. 2) regs. 1967 [S.I. 1967 No. 1572].

Chapter Three

CONFUSION

The period of five years from 1971 to 1975 (inclusive) was one of very great legislative activity in the national insurance field. Some 15 statutes were enacted, or more according to how one defines the field. And it was during this period, particularly towards the end of it, that confusion crept in, due to an intention apparently to discard the well-understood phrase "national insurance" and to substitute for it something else. The difficulty is to see what that something else was.

The Ministry of Social Security Act 1966 [1] changed the name of the ministry from the Ministry of Pensions and National Insurance to the Ministry of Social Security, which later became part of the Department of Health and Social Security.[2] It also caused national assistance to be replaced by supplementary benefit, payable like other benefits by that ministry, thus introducing the word "benefit" into the area which previously had been known as that of the Poor Law or National Assistance. Moreover as time went on the phrase "social security" gradually came in common parlance to mean or at least to include supplementary benefit, though social security benefits had not yet become a statutory phrase. There was therefore a considerable risk of confusion if that phrase were used to describe what had hitherto been called national insurance benefits either with or without industrial injuries benefits but excluding supplementary benefit.[3] Where numerous benefits under different sets of statutes are administered by different sets of adjudicating authorities, and the same event may result in a payment which is not benefit at all as well as a right to benefit, it is and always was essential that there should be words to distinguish clearly between each benefit, each group, great or small, of benefits, and any other payments. Down to and for some time after the three consolidating Acts of 1965 this was achieved. National insurance benefits meant benefits provided by the National Insurance Acts using that phrase in the narrow sense excluding the Industrial Injuries Acts. The phraseology became completely accepted and everyone understood what it meant, even after the amalgamation effected by the National Insurance Act 1966. Abbreviations were based on it. The National Insurance Advisory Committee became known as "NIAC," and national insurance local tribunals as "NILTs."[4] Industrial injuries (or injury) benefits meant benefits under the Industrial Injuries Acts, even though those Acts contained the words national insurance in their short titles. The phrase family allowances meant what it said. All these were clearly distinguishable from each other and from national assistance, supplementary benefit and damages at common law.

In 1971, in addition to the National Insurance Act 1971, which dealt mainly with national insurance and industrial injuries, there was a Social Security Act 1971. It dealt mainly with supplementary benefit, but it also made some changes in the law of national insurance and industrial injuries. In 1972 three further statutes with short titles containing the words "national insurance" were enacted.[5] The year 1973 saw the enactment of the Social Security Act 1973, a massive statute containing 288 pages, over 100 sections and 28 Schedules.[6] The long title of the Act began: "An Act to establish a basic scheme of social security contributions and benefits replacing the National Insurance Acts, . . ." Chapter II of Part I began by providing that: "Basic scheme benefits shall be of the following descriptions," and it went on to list with the utmost clarity what had been national insurance benefits under the 1946 and 1965 Acts, together with subsequent additions.[7] The rest of Chapter 2 set out the conditions of title to those benefits, broadly speaking on the lines of the existing legislation.[8] So far as I recall the phrase "national insurance benefit" appeared nowhere in the 1973 Act, though the National Insurance Advisory Committee, the National Insurance Fund and the National Insurance Commissioners continued to be referred to in it by those names. From this it seems clear that in 1973 the intention was that those benefits which previously had been known as national insurance benefits should now be known as either basic scheme benefits or basic scheme social security benefits. The phrase " national insurance " was on the way out. Other Parts of the 1973 Act contained important provisions relating to pensions, and provided for the setting up of the Occupational Pensions Board. The Act entrusted to the Board the decision of certain questions, as indeed earlier legislation had to the Registrar and Adjudicator,[9] but I need not refer further to them, since the exercise of their powers in no way overlapped or affected those of the statutory authorities. The 1973 Act did not deal otherwise than incidentally with any questions of adjudication relating to industrial injuries benefits; the Industrial Injuries Act 1965 and the National Insurance Act 1966 were to continue to govern that field. Most of the 1973 Act was intended not to come into operation before April 6, 1975, and meanwhile the administration of the benefits as national insurance benefits continued as before under the 1965 legislation as supplemented by later Acts. The phrases " basic scheme benefits " or " basic scheme social security benefits " made no immediate impact.[10]

The appointed day for the benefit provisions in the 1973 Act having not yet arrived,[11] Parliament continued to legislate for national insurance under that name. In 1973 it enacted the National Insurance and Supplementary Benefit Act 1973 and the Pensioners' Payments and National Insurance Act 1973. Further Acts were passed in 1974. The long title of one of them, the National Insurance Act 1974, perhaps throws light on the meaning of the phrase " social security." The phrase in it " to make minor amendments of certain other enactments relating to social security " appears to relate to section 6 of the Act, the marginal note of which reads: " Minor supplementary provisions and amendments of certain social security enactments." This section enabled regulations to be made creating a " slip rule " and providing for the setting aside of decisions in certain circumstances. The statutes to which this rule was to relate included the National Insurance Acts, the Industrial Injuries Acts, the Family Allowances Acts, the Supplementary Benefits Acts, the Family Income Supplements Act and the Social Security Act 1973. The phrase social security was therefore here being used in a very wide sense and certainly not simply as a substitute for "national insurance."

The Social Security Amendment Act 1974 however was clearly looking forward to the date when the benefit provisions in the 1973 Act were to come into force and to the consolidations which were being prepared. A marginal note in it referred to a section of the 1965 Act as "social security legislation." [12]

The last statute enacted in this field before the big 1975 consolidations was the Social Security Benefits Act 1975. This Act threw light on both the wide meaning of the phrase "social security" and also the use of the phrase "basic scheme benefits" as the modern equivalent of national insurance benefits. The Act dealt with basic scheme benefits, describing them repeatedly by that name, and with benefits in respect of industrial injuries and diseases, family allowances and supplementary benefit. It created two new basic scheme benefits to be included among those in section 9 (1) of the Social Security Act 1973, namely non-contributory invalidity pension and invalid care allowance.[13] The sections creating these two new benefits had not come into force by April 6, 1975, the date of the consolidations, but the sections providing for the two new benefits are reproduced in the Social Security Act 1975.[14]

This brings us to the 1975 consolidations, which for Great Britain are the Social Security Act 1975 and the Industrial Injuries and Diseases (Old Cases) Act 1975, the latter of which I am disregarding for the reasons already explained.[15] Ancillary provisions are contained in the Social Security (Consequential Provisions) Act 1975.

The long title of the Social Security Act 1975 reads: "An Act to consolidate for England, Wales and Scotland so much of the Social Security Act 1973 as establishes a basic scheme of contributions and benefits, together with the National Insurance (Industrial Injuries) Acts 1965 to 1974 and other enactments relating to social security." Part II of the Act consolidates the benefit provisions contained in the Social Security Act 1973 with later additions and the industrial injuries benefit provisions in the Industrial Injuries Act 1965. Part III consolidates the provisions governing the determination of claims and questions, and Part IV consolidates administrative provisions contained in earlier Acts. One effect of the Act is to complete the merger, which had been started by the National Insurance Act 1966, of the administration of what used to be national insurance and industrial injuries benefits. Surprisingly, however, I can find no reference anywhere in the Social Security Act 1975 after the long title to either the "basic scheme" or "basic scheme benefits." The reference in the Consequential Provisions Act 1975, s. 3 (3), to: "transition from old system of national insurance to new system of social security" confirms the impression derived from many sources of an intention on the part of the legislature to get rid of the phrase "national insurance."

The 1975 Act provides the benefits formerly provided by the 1946 and 1965 Acts as national insurance benefits, and referred to in the 1973 Act as basic scheme benefits, but unfortunately it nowhere indicates by what name they are to be called in the 1975 Act. Calling them "contributory" [16] or "short-term" [17] does not tell us what sort of benefits they are. If they are to be known as social security benefits from the title of the Act providing them, nothing could be more confusing, since for a long time that phrase had been used as meaning or including supplementary benefits and perhaps other benefits under other legislation. Industrial injuries benefits provided under the same part of the same Act (the 1975 Act) are separately defined in the Act, and are apparently not basic scheme benefits.[18]

Before April 6, 1975, much of the law had been in regulations contained in statutory instruments, whose titles began with the words "national insurance" or "national insurance (industrial injuries)" and continued with words in brackets indicating the subject-matter. With effect from April 6, 1975, most of these have been revoked and replaced by new statutory instruments, the titles of which contain the words "social security" instead. Some of these relate only to benefits which previously were national insurance benefits,[19] others to industrial injuries benefits only,[20] others to both former national insurance and industrial injuries benefits, though the title gives no indication of this.[21] Regulations relating to supplementary benefit or family allowances indicate this clearly, though the words " social security " appear between the number of the statutory instrument and its title, as they had done for a considerable time before.[22]

The words " basic scheme " crept timidly into the headings of a statutory instrument in 1973 and two in 1974, but I have not noticed them since.[23] The Social Security (Correction and Setting Aside of Decisions) Regulations 1975 [24] made under powers to which I have already referred suggest that social security has a very wide meaning indeed.[25]

In the 1975 Act, as in the 1973 Act, the phrase " national insurance " survives in the titles of the National Insurance Advisory Committee, the National Insurance Fund and the National Insurance Commissioners.[26] The 1975 Act, however, contains no reference to national insurance benefits. It therefore seems surprising to find many Department of Health and Social Security leaflets issued for use after April 5, 1975, continuing to describe benefits as national insurance benefits. I have noticed more than 15 such leaflets. They still all have distinguishing numbers prefaced by the letters " NI," and some of them imply that national insurance benefits and supplementary benefit are two species of the genus social security benefits.[27]

I think that the general public continued to use the phrase " social security " as including (or meaning) supplementary benefit and excluding what had been national insurance benefits. A number of legal publications and the media continued after April 1975 still to treat the topics with which I am concerned under the heading of national insurance, and to regard social security as meaning supplementary benefit. In August 1975 there was on BBC television a debate in two parts entitled " Is it right that Social Security Benefits should be paid to strikers' families? " [28] The discussion could not have related to unemployment benefit or an increase of it and was correctly treated throughout as relating to supplementary benefit.[29]

In some publications the writer has used the phrase social security ambiguously as meaning sometimes national insurance and sometimes supplementary benefit, it being difficult or impossible to tell which he is referring to at any given moment. In these circumstances, a reference as early as May 1975 in the Legal Action Group's Bulletin to social security being now the term for national insurance seems to me to have been very perceptive.

It must be remembered that owing to the manner in which the 1975 Act was brought into force the benefit provisions of the 1973 Act, which introduced the phrase " basic scheme " benefits, were in force for only an infinitely short time. Those provisions were among the ones referred to in section 3 (1) of the Consequential Provisions Act 1975. They came into force on April 6, 1975,[30] but as soon as they had done so the 1975 Act itself came into force, and the benefit provisions of the 1973 Act were repealed together with the whole of the 1965 Act and the Industrial Injuries Act 1965. Here again there is evidence of an intention to get rid of the phrase " national insurance." Section 3 (3) of the Consequential Provisions Act has already been mentioned.[31] A reference to that Act, Schedule 1, Part I reminds us that a number of Acts which had made incidental references to statutes in our field now contained the words " national insurance and social security," these words in some instances having been inserted by the 1973 Act.[32] The Consequential Provisions Act 1975 now deleted the words " national insurance and," which suggests that the words " social security " were intended to have a very wide interpretation.[33]

I am afraid that in other ways confusion has been created, which is not merely temporary during a transitional period, but permanent until it is altered. Consolidation should be complete. The result of it should be that, once disputes arising during any transitional period have been dealt with, nobody need look at the earlier provisions because they have been repealed and replaced by the consolidating legislation. One needs only to look, however, at Schedule 1 to the Consequential Provisions Act 1975 to see that the repeals of the earlier legislation, for example the 1973 Act, are selective. I have not examined that Schedule in detail to ascertain how much of the 1973 Act is left, but can illustrate the point by one example. The 1973 Act, section 99 subsection (18) as amended provides: " The Ministry of Social Security Act 1966 is cited in this Act as the Supplementary Benefit Act 1966 and may be so cited in any other Act instrument or document." [34] Obviously the change in 1973 of the name of a statute which came into force in 1966 carries with it a severe risk of inconvenience. If one looks in the 1966 statutes for a Supplementary Benefit Act one will not find one. If Parliament decides to change the name of a statute, however, in my opinion it should do so thoroughly. In this case it has not. Whatever exactly may be covered by the words " instrument or document " they would certainly not cover counsel's oral argument in court, so counsel strictly speaking could not use the new name; I express no opinion on whether it would cover a written judgment delivered orally in court. In saying this, however, I have slipped into using the present tense. Is this provision still in force, and if not has it been replaced, and if so where? This involves considering three questions: whether it was ever brought into force and if so how, whether it has been repealed, and if so where it has been re-enacted. The 1973 Act was brought into force by four commencement orders [35] and there was another order which revoked parts of the earlier ones.[36] An examination of the orders shows that section 99 came into operation in July 1973. The Consequential Provisions Act 1975, Schedule 1 does not mention subsection (18), so it is not repealed there, and so far as I know it is not repealed elsewhere. The result is that despite the consolidation anyone needing to refer to this provision has to find it in the 1973 Act (as amended), which most of us I suppose had believed would be entirely consolidated into the 1975 Act. As there have been several Acts of Parliament since 1973 dealing with supplementary benefit perhaps that would have been the best place to put the provision.

Another curiosity in the location of an amendment is to be found in the repeal of part of section 19 of the 1975 Act by the Employment Protection Act 1975.[37]

All in all, you may perhaps agree with me that the title of this chapter " Confusion " is amply justified. Parliament has made it tolerably clear that it has decided to get rid of the phrase "national insurance" for some purposes, but it has not made clear what is to be put in its place. The Department in its literature has for some 10 months after the coming into force of the 1975 Act continued to refer to national insurance benefits by that name. In the circumstances, although it may be technically incorrect, I shall do the same. These matters affected the choice of a title for my lectures. Their subject is the Commissioners and their work. There is however no convenient phrase which includes that work but excludes everything else. So I chose for these lectures the title that I did, despite a grave warning from a retired judge that if I called them "The National Insurance Commissioners" nobody would come. The judge thereby unconsciously demonstrated the lofty attitude of many conventional lawyers towards tribunals in general and this branch of the law in particular.

As to the future, it is a sad reflection that one phrase which has up to now been completely unambiguous, a family allowance, will be replaced by the phrase child benefit, with all the risk of confusion between that and the increases of benefit in respect of children under the 1975 Act if they continue to exist.

Notes

[1] See also pp. 28 and 100, n. 68.

[2] See the Secretary of State for Social Services Order 1968 [S.I. 1968 No. 1699].

[3] There always had been a danger of confusion, which had to be guarded against, between the genus industrial injuries (or injury) benefits and the species industrial injury benefit.

[4] There was no corresponding abbreviation for National Insurance Commissioners, so far as I know.

[5] See the National Insurance (Amendment) Act 1972, the National Insurance Act 1972 and the Pensioners' Payments and National Insurance Contributions Act 1972.

[6] Some of the provisions referred only to Northern Ireland.

[7] See the 1973 Act, s. 9.

[8] The phrases "the basic scheme" and "basic scheme benefits" were defined in the 1973 Act, s. 99 (1).

[9] See the N.I. Act 1965, s. 74.

[10] At the time when the 1973 Act was enacted there were a number of statutes (dealing with other matters) containing references to the

1946 Act and the I.I. Act 1946. The 1973 Act (Sched. 27, Pt. I) amended these provisions, in a number of instances substituting the words "enactments relating to national insurance and social security."

[11] Owing to the change of government between its enactment and April 1975 important parts of the Act never did take effect.

[12] See the S.S. Amendment Act 1974, s. 5.

[13] See the S.S. Benefits Act 1975, ss. 5, 6 and 7.

[14] See the 1975 Act, ss. 36 and 37. See further p. 91, below.

[15] See p. 19, n. 12.

[16] See the 1975 Act, Pt. II, Chap. I.

[17] See the 1975 Act, Sched. 20.

[18] See the 1975 Act, s. 50. The definition of benefit in Sched. 20 does not help.

[19] *e.g.* the S.S. (Death Grant) regs. 1975 [S.I. 1975 No. 565].

[20] *e.g.* the S.S. (Industrial Injuries) (Benefit) regs. 1975 [S.I. 1975 No. 559].

[21] *e.g.* the S.S. (Claims and Payments) regs. 1975 [S.I. 1975 No. 560] and the S.S. (D.C.Q.) regs. 1975 [S.I. 1975 No. 558].

[22] *e.g.*, the Supplementary Benefit (Determination of Requirements) regs. 1975 [S.I. 1975 No. 464]. The title of the S.S. and F.A. (Polygamous Marriages) regs. 1975 [S.I. 1975 No. 561] suggests that family allowances are something different from social security benefits.

[23] See S.I. 1973 No. 1376; S.I. 1974 No. 141 and S.I. 1974 No. 2009.

[24] See S.I. 1975 No. 572.

[25] See the N.I. Act 1974, s. 6 (1) and p. 23, above.

[26] See the 1975 Act, ss. 138, 133 and 97.

[27] See, *e.g.* leaflets N.I. 209/Nov. 1975, N.I. 155A and 205 (Dec. 1975) and N.I. 146 (Jan. 1976).

[28] See the *Radio Times* for Aug. 2–8 and 9–15, 1975.

[29] See also p. 34, below.

[30] See the S.S. Act 1973 (Commencement No. 2) Order 1973 [S.I. 1973 No. 1433 (C. 40)].

[31] See p. 25, above.

[32] See n. 10, above.

[33] Lord Justice Scarman (see p. 138, below) and Professor Calvert (see p. 7, above) treat social security as a generic term including national insurance and supplementary benefit.

[34] The words "instrument or document" were substituted for "or instrument" by the N.I. Act 1974, s. 6 (5) and Sched. 4, para. 28. *Cf.* p. 20, n. 28, above, see also p. 34, below.

[35] S.I. 1973 No. 1249 (C. 30); S.I. 1973 No. 1433 (C. 40); S.I. 1974 No. 164 (C. 3) and S.I. 1975 No. 124 (C. 2).

[36] S.I. 1974 No. 823 (C. 14).

[37] Employment Protection Act 1975, s. 111. That section is not yet in force; it is not one of those which came into force early in 1976 by virtue of the Employment Protection Act 1975 (Commencement No. 1) Order 1975 [S.I. 1975 No. 1938 (C. 55)].

Chapter Four

SPECIAL FEATURES OF NATIONAL INSURANCE LAW

Substantive Law

At hearings it is sometimes obvious that the claimant's representative has no idea of the general principles, which constitute the skeleton supporting the individual provisions which are the flesh and blood of this body of law. It may therefore be helpful if I indicate some of the main characteristics of Social Security Act law which distinguish it from other more familiar branches of the law.

The benefits provided are not payable unless certain statutory conditions are fulfilled. The statutes and the numerous regulations under them are intended to constitute a code containing the whole of the law. There is no such thing as a common law of social security or national insurance. Equitable doctrines are relevant only in so far as they affect the interpretation of the statutes and regulations. It is therefore pointless to argue that although the claimant does not quite satisfy the statutory conditions he so nearly does so that it would be equitable to grant him the benefit.[1]

In most branches of the law if you are entitled to something and claim it in appropriate proceedings within a fairly long statutory period of limitation you will be awarded it. This is not necessarily so under the 1975 Act. For most of the benefits there are three obstacles to success and for some of them two. You may fail to satisfy the statutory conditions and so be disentitled. Even if you are entitled, however, you may be disqualified. And even if you are entitled and not disqualified, benefit may not be payable. For example, a man who has contributed to the national insurance scheme all his working life attains the age of 70 but, enjoying good health and believing that to get a retirement pension he must have retired, he continues to work drawing a substantial salary for another 18 months before retiring and claiming. He is then astonished to learn that on becoming 70 he was " deemed " to have retired although in fact he had not done so,[2] and he could have been awarded a retirement pension from his seventieth birthday despite the size of his earnings. The prescribed time for claiming his pension, however, was and is only three months.[3] His claim in respect of three months before the date when he did claim is therefore allowed, but he is held by the insurance officer to be disqualified in respect of any earlier period because he has not shown good cause for the delay in claiming.[4] He indignantly appeals to the local tribunal, where after further investigation it is accepted that there was good cause for the delay. The local tribunal, however, can only award the benefit for a further nine months because the absolute time limit in the Act of 12 months for claiming provides that no sum shall be paid to any person on account of benefit for any period more than 12 months before the date on which the claim is made.[5] So in respect of six of the 18 months he is entitled and not disqualified but the money is not payable.

A feature of national insurance law also relating to time which many people find confusing is that benefit is not always payable, apart from any questions of disqualification, etc., for all the days during which the events giving rise to the claim subsist. This is illustrated by the rules governing title to unemployment and sickness benefit, which are contained partly in the Act and partly in regulations.[6] The idea behind the main rules governing these benefits in the Act is that neither benefit is to be payable for a single, isolated day or even for a very short, isolated period, but that in calculating the days the two benefits are treated together almost as if they were one and the same benefit. The machinery by which effect is given to these ideas is briefly as follows. Neither benefit is payable except for a day of interruption of employment, which means a day of unemployment or of incapacity for work, and the day of interruption of employment must form part of a period of interruption of employment.[7] Such a period must itself consist of at least two days (not necessarily consecutive) within a period of six days (excluding Sundays). Also any two periods of interruption of employment separated by not more than

13 weeks are treated as one period of interruption of employment.[8] These rules for lumping together days and periods assume a special importance in conjunction with another rule by which there is no title to either of the two benefits for the first three days of a period of interruption of employment.[9] It is obviously advantageous to claimants to have as few as possible of these periods of three days. This all seems very complicated, but there is worse to come. The regulations set out a number of circumstances in which a day is not to be treated as a day of unemployment or incapacity for work, with the result that benefit is not payable for that day, and it does not count towards the three days. The fairly commonly held view that to obtain unemployment benefit all you need is to have contributed and to be in fact out of work is therefore incorrect. These rules are in effect incorporated into the industrial injuries scheme in relation to injury benefit.[10] Similar considerations apply to invalidity benefit; to avoid further complication I have disregarded them.

Pausing here for a moment, I think that this notion of benefit not being payable for a day which cannot by law be "treated" as a day of unemployment needs further consideration. It creates a legal fiction, and if my experience has taught me anything it is that legal fictions are unacceptable to Miss Hamlyn's Common People. If the law tells a man that whilst unemployed he cannot be paid benefit unless he satisfies certain conditions, that is something that he can understand even if he does not like it. If he tells him, however, that a day cannot be treated as a day of unemployment when he knows all too well that in fact it was, that is something against which he revolts.

Benefit always consists of a payment in money or in the form of a voucher which can be exchanged for money; it is never provided in kind. Sometimes it takes the form of a single payment.[11] More commonly it consists of periodical, often weekly, payments, which are indexed. Various statutory devices make these extremely flexible, which in my opinion gives the system, especially in an age of inflation, a vast advantage over some other systems where the award is a once-for-all award of a lump sum.

A man with no dependants may be entitled to benefit at a certain rate. This is known as personal benefit.[12] The personal rate may however be increased, for example where the claimant has a wife or other adult dependant or children or both. This convenient arrangement did not, however, fit in easily with other practices. Most wages do not take account of the size of the employee's family. Increases of benefit do. These two facts taken together created a most intractable problem. A man with a very large family could be actually better off drawing benefit than working. If offered a job which brought in less than the benefit, was it reasonable for him to refuse it? A Tribunal of Commissioners had to deal with this problem many years ago,[13] but the introduction of the family income supplement has now affected the situation. Whether the Child Benefit Act 1975 or regulations under it will affect it further and if so how remains to be seen. Child benefit will of course differ from an increase of unemployment benefit, just as a family allowance already does—in relation to strikes; a family allowance is not affected if the loss of employment comes within the trade dispute section of the 1975 Act,[14] whereas if a person is disqualified for receiving personal unemployment benefit under that section he is equally disqualified for receiving any increases of it.

There are many other devices to provide for different circumstances. The normal ("basic") rate of benefit may be increased, for example by means of an earnings-related supplement to some benefits,[15] or increases of retirement pension for pensioners who continue to work after pensionable age.[16] Or it may be reduced for insufficient contributions,[17] or if a retirement pensioner within five years after pensionable age works and earns too much.[18]

In the industrial injuries field, further flexibility is achieved in awarding disablement benefit by the additional devices by which the degree of disablement is assessed (by the medical authorities) in the form of a percentage ranging from 1 per cent. to 100 per cent., on the basis of which benefit is awarded by the statutory authorities,[19] and also by having available a further series of increases of benefit related to particular consequences of the disability.[20]

Still further flexibility is produced by the power to review the decisions of the various adjudicating authorities.[21]

I believe that the number and variety of these provisions is one of the greatest strengths of the system, since they enable vastly different awards appropriate to vastly different circumstances to be made by persons not skilled in the very fine art of assessing general damages.

A fact frequently overlooked is that need is never the condition or even a condition of title to benefit under the 1975 Act, though of course it may be a result of circumstances which do create a title. Conversely wealth does not disentitle. A millionaire may draw unemployment benefit, if he is an employed earner (provided that hardly any of his income is earned), or a retirement pension.[22]

Procedure

I now turn to procedure. The first thing to be noted is that the times for claiming are extremely short, far shorter than those with which lawyers are familiar in many other spheres. Most of them appear not in the 1975 Act itself but in regulations.[23] Thus unemployment benefit must be claimed on the very first day of unemployment; otherwise some benefit may be lost. The time can be extended within limits if good cause for the delay is proved, but it is by no means easy to prove.[23] There is however a compensating feature. Delay does not destroy the cause of action altogether, as it does in many other spheres. It merely limits the period which an award can cover. A person can therefore theoretically be awarded disablement benefit for an accident which happened 25 years ago if he can succeed in proving that the accident happened at all. The award will however cover a period not earlier than three months before the date of the claim unless he proves good cause for the delay in claiming.

The adjudication system differs fundamentally from those of most other branches of the law in respect of the distribution among various authorities of the duty in deciding questions. In some branches of the law we are accustomed to this up to a point, so much so that we hardly notice it. An obvious example is trial by jury. There there is a difference, however, the judge has a considerable degree of control over the jury. If there is no or no sufficient evidence to support a particular verdict, the judge will direct the jury accordingly, and they will obey his direction. The 1975 Act system is different. Once any determining authority has decided a question entrusted to it for decision, that decision is (subject to s. 117 of the 1975 Act) binding absolutely on any other determining authority, no matter at what level the decision has been made.[24]

The duty of deciding whether and to what extent the contribution conditions for a benefit are satisfied is by statute entrusted to the Secretary of State.[25] Once she (of course through one of the officers of the department authorised by her) has given a decision on a contribution question, that decision is absolutely binding on the statutory authorities including a Commissioner, who has no power to entertain evidence or argument designed to contradict it. He must simply accept it. It is therefore completely pointless for a claimant or his representative to try to persuade the statutory authorities that the Secretary of State's decision on a matter entrusted to her for decision is incorrect.[26] The Commissioners therefore have jurisdiction to cover only half the ground. Broadly speaking they are concerned with the question whether a particular sum shall be paid out to a claimant, and also sometimes whether a claimant has been overpaid and should be required to refund.[27] They have no jurisdiction, however, to decide how much the claimant has contributed or must contribute.

Three matters which are frequently misunderstood should be mentioned. Many claimants think that a Commissioner has a much wider discretion to award benefit than the insurance officer or the local tribunal. This is not so. The questions for decision by the statutory authorities at all levels are identical.

Secondly, solicitors sometimes ask for an interview with the Department, the insurance officer or even the Commissioner, with a view to negotiating a settlement of a claim. Such a proposal is completely misconceived. The question for decision is whether the claimant does or does not satisfy the conditions for the receipt of a particular statutory benefit. Either he does or he does not. The Commissioners have always taken the view that no question of settlement arises.

Thirdly, the argument is sometimes put forward by a claimant, particularly during a strike, that someone, whom I will call Mr. A., worked in the same factory as the claimant and was laid off with him during a strike, and has been awarded benefit; that Mr. A.'s case is identical with the claimant's; and that therefore the claimant's claim should not have been disallowed. Whether or not the appeal succeeds on other grounds, this is a contention which cannot prevail. Without knowing every detail of Mr. A.'s case, which is not before the statutory authorities in the present case, and the grounds for the disallowance of the claimant's claim it is impossible to say whether the two cases are in truth identical. The claimant may be disqualified for receiving benefit for some reason which does not apply to Mr. A.; for example he (or at present some member of his grade or class)[28] was directly interested in the dispute or (at present) he was financing it through his union but Mr. A. was not. Another possibility is that Mr. A. was wrongly awarded benefit, perhaps in a different district, where the consequences of the strike differed, or because the facts of the case were not fully known. In such cases claimants tend always to assume that the favourable decision was correct and the unfavourable one was not. Another possibility is that the cases raise difficult questions of law, as indeed they do when one gets disputed questions about the combination of a strike, short-term working, and guaranteed week clauses. On such questions there is always the possibility of adjudicating authorities taking different views of the law. In such cases the proper course for the statutory authority is to decide the claimant's case on the basis of the law as they understand it, on the facts of the claimant's case, and not on what are said to be the facts of some other case. Of course if it has been agreed that one case shall be treated as a test case for others then the decision in them will be governed by the test case. It is most important, however, that there should be a clear understanding as to what other cases are to be governed by the test case.[29] It is of course most unfortunate that there should be different decisions in apparently similar cases; but if the two cases really are indistinguishable and the insurance officer in the claimants' case thinks that the decision in Mr. A.'s case was incorrect, there may be no effective means of challenging the latter [30]; moreover even if there is, if the benefit has been paid and is irrecoverable such proceedings leading to a different result would be a waste of public time and money.

The provisions entrusting the decision of different questions to different authorities, coupled with the further provision that their decisions are final,[31] were bound to raise questions as to the meaning and extent of the finality of decisions. The problem arose as early as 1950, when a Tribunal of Commissioners held that " final " meant merely final as regards the claim for benefit in respect of which the decision was given.[32] This decision governed the situation for many years. However, the view expressed in it was inconsistent with the decision of the House of Lords in the *Dowling* case, after which many problems arose both before and after the subsequent *Hudson* and *Jones* cases.[33] Parliament then stepped in and dealt with the problem by legislation.[34]

Notes

[1] Doctrines evolved in other branches of the law may of course be relevant, *e.g. res judicata*: see Decision R(I) 9/63, paras. 24 and 25.

[2] See Chap. 9, below, especially p. 113.

[3] S.S. (Claims and Payments) regs. 1975 [S.I. 1975 No. 560], Sched. 1, para. 5.

[4] S.S. (Claims and Payments) regs. 1975 [S.I. 1975 No. 560], reg. 13 (2).

[5] The 1975 Act, s. 82 (2) (*c*).

[6] See the 1975 Act, ss. 14 and 17, and the S.S. (U.S.I. Benefit) regs. 1975 [S.I. 1975 No. 564], especially reg. 7.

[7] Commonly referred to as a " p.i.e." See the 1975 Act, s. 14 (1) (*a*).

[8] See the 1975 Act, s. 17 (1) (*d*).

[9] This rule is now absolute; see the 1975 Act, s. 15 (1) concluding words. Formerly it was qualified; see the 1965 Act, s. 19 (6), but the

qualification was repealed by the S.S. Act 1971, s. 7 (1). These three days used to be called "waiting days."

[10] See the 1975 Act, s. 56 (4).

[11] *e.g.*, a grant under the 1975 Act, Sched. 4, Pt. II or a disablement gratuity under s. 57 (5).

[12] The phrase "personal benefit" is not defined or used much if at all in the Act, but it plays an important part in the rules governing overlapping; see the S.S. (Overlapping Benefits) regs. 1975 [S.I. 1975 No. 554], where it is defined. Two benefits are said to overlap if they are awarded for the same event, as industrial injury benefit and sickness benefit are for incapacity for work. If they overlap the beneficiary is paid only one of them. See further p. 99, n. 54.

[13] See Decision R(U) 10/61.

[14] See the 1975 Act, s. 19.

[15] See the 1975 Act, s. 14 (7).

[16] See s. 28.

[17] See s. 33.

[18] See s. 30. Whether it will be sensible to continue to refer to a retirement pension by that name as opposed to an old age pension when section 30 (2) takes effect fully may depend mainly on the rate of inflation.

[19] Many people, even lawyers, believe that disablement benefit is *awarded* by the medical authorities. It is not.

[20] See the 1975 Act, ss. 57–66.

[21] See the 1975 Act, ss. 104, 106 and 110.

[22] An important difference between them is that the former is not taxable whereas the latter is; see the Income and Corporation Taxes Act 1970, s. 219 as amended. For those in need, supplementary benefit and family income supplement may be available, but they are not part of the subject-matter of these lectures.

[23] See the S.S. (Claims and Payment) regs. 1975 [S.I. 1975 No. 560], reg. 13 and Sched. 1. The absolute time limit is in the 1975 Act, s. 82 (2). The Department have issued a series of most useful leaflets explaining different matters in simple terms. So far as I can remember there has never been one on time limits. Nor do I remember having ever heard a radio talk about them. From the very numerous appeals which come before Commissioners relating to late claims and the obvious feeling of injustice experienced by many claimants I think that taking either of these steps might well be worthy of consideration.

[24] Thus a decision by an insurance officer may be binding on a medical appeal tribunal, even though it may relate to medical questions.

[25] The 1975 Act, s. 93.

[26] It may be proper and reasonable to invite the statutory authority to refer a contribution question back to the Secretary of State under s. 103, though this is something which the claimant can in effect do himself under the S.S. (D.C.Q.) regs. 1975 [S.I. 1975 No. 558],

reg. 8. Questions relating to contributions, etc., are for decision by the Secretary of State and not the statutory authorities (see the 1975 Act, s. 93). Where it would assist in reaching a decision, a member of the staff of the Department's Solicitor's Office is appointed to hold an oral inquiry (see the D.H.S.S. Annual Report 1974, Cmnd. 6150, para. 10.12, p. 103). There is no right of appeal from such a decision on questions of fact, though there is on law under the 1975 Act, s. 94. Mr. Crossman's 1969–70 Bill included a clause (74) which, though it did not create an actual right of appeal against a Secretary of State's decision, provided that the latter " may " refer the question to a special tribunal. The Council on Tribunals preferred an appeal to the existing statutory authorities rather than the creation of a new tribunal. (See the Council's Reports for 1969–70, para. 47 and Appendix B, containing the Chairman's letter of Feb. 27, 1970 to the Lord Chancellor, and 1970–71, Appendix A, containing a further letter of July 20, 1970, also to the Lord Chancellor.) The Bill was never enacted.

[27] Where a decision is reversed or varied on appeal or revised on a review, money paid under the original decision is not repayable if the claimant has used due care and diligence to avoid overpayment. See the 1975 Act, s. 119; formerly the 1965 Act, s. 81 and the I.I. Act 1965, s. 54. Originally the test was not due care and diligence, but (under regulations) good faith. This was a less exacting test for claimants to comply with, but it caused immense resentment when they failed to do so.

[28] See the 1975 Act, s. 19. The " grade or class " and " financing " provisions in the 1975 Act, s. 19 are to be repealed by the Employment Protection Act 1975, s. 111; see p. 30, n. 37.

[29] As to test cases and test questions, see Decision R(U) 7/71.

[30] An insurance officer has no right of appeal against an insurance officer's decision to a local tribunal under the 1975 Act, s. 100, and there may or may not be grounds for review under s. 104. Recovery of sums overpaid is governed by s. 119.

[31] See, *e.g.*, the I.I. Acts 1946, s. 36 (3) and 1965, s. 50 (1).

[32] Decision C.I. 438/50 (reported).

[33] See the speech of Lord Hodson, with whose reasons Lord Reid and Lord Guest agreed, in the *Dowling* case [1967] 1 A.C. 725 at p. 750E and the speeches in *Jones* v. *Secretary of State for Social Services* [1972] A.C. 944.

[34] See the N.I. Act 1972, s. 5, now replaced by the 1975 Act, s. 117.

CHAPTER FIVE

THE COMMISSIONERS

I now turn to the question what exactly a Commissioner is.[1] The expression " Commissioner " is defined in the 1975 Act as meaning, unless the context otherwise requires (which it never does) the Chief National Insurance Commissioner, or any other National Insurance Commissioner, including a Tribunal of three Commissioners.[2] The Act provides that Her Majesty the Queen may from time to time appoint, from among persons who are barristers or advocates of not less than 10 years' standing, a Chief National Insurance Commissioner and such number of other National Insurance Commissioners as Her Majesty may think fit.[3] The appointment of a Commissioner is contained in a document signed in Her Majesty's own handwriting, countersigned by the Lord Chancellor and bearing the seal of the Crown Office.[4] The appointment is during good behaviour.[5] It does not specify any period, but on appointment a Commissioner gives an undertaking to tender his resignation at the end of the year of service in which he attains the age of 72. The Act does not say whether the appointment is to be whole-time or part-time. All the present Commissioners hold full-time appointments, though some of them and others formerly held part-time ones. The Act provides for a Commissioner to be paid a salary and expenses by the Secretary of State,[6] and a pension may be awarded on her recommendation.[7] The decision as to the amount rests with the Minister for the Civil Service. Although the Secretary of State and the Department and all their predecessors have in my experience always acted with the most scrupulous correctness in respect of the salaries and pensions of Commissioners, I have always thought that on principle the payment of the salary and the recommendation for a pension ought to be made by the Lord Chancellor rather than by the Secretary of State.

Some of the present Commissioners were appointed as Deputy National Insurance Commissioners (and also Deputy Industrial

Injuries Commissioners) under the 1946 Legislation but their offices were converted into those of National Insurance Commissioners by the National Insurance Act 1966, s. 9. Others were appointed under that section. The present Chief Commissioner, Mr. R. J. A. Temple Q.C., was appointed as such under section 97 of the 1975 Act, having previously been a Commissioner appointed under section 9 of the 1966 Act. As the *Law List* does not anywhere give the names of the Commissioners other than the Chief Commissioner I have recorded in a note [8] the names of the present ones and some of their predecessors. This seems desirable, since persons who were "inferior tribunals" are soon forgotten. Many of us know that before the days of the Commissioners unemployment benefit appeals were decided by someone called the Umpire. But how many of us could say who he was or would know where to look to find out?

Upon appointment each Commissioner becomes in law a statutory tribunal and consequently under the direct supervision of the Council on Tribunals. This is clear from the Tribunals and Inquiries Act 1971.[9] Collectively the Commissioners form the top tier of the three-tier statutory authority adjudicating structure. A Commissioner is appointed for the whole of Great Britain and not for England or Scotland or Wales only. His jurisdiction is entirely appellate and not original,[10] and is now governed by three sections of the Act and regulations relating to appeals from local tribunals, medical appeal tribunals and the Attendance Allowance Board respectively,[11] together with section 5 as amended of the Family Allowances Act 1965. In the *Jones* case (1962) [12] Lord Parker C.J. described a Commissioner as "a quasi-judicial tribunal deciding a case *inter partes.*" I hope that some day many tribunals including the Commissioners will be universally recognised as performing judicial duties. We certainly aimed at achieving something better than quasi-justice. The Legislature has used other words to describe the Commissioners. In the Acts and regulations they have been at different times included in the terms "insurance tribunal," [13] "adjudicating authority," [14] "adjudicating officials and bodies," [15] "determining authorities" [16] and "competent tribunal."[17] My experience is that in practice nobody uses any of these expressions. The statutory authorities are referred to by that name, and the medical board and medical appeal tribunal as the medical authorities.[18]

As to the status of a Commissioner, if salary is any guide to this it will be noted that the Report on Top Salaries recommended for the Chief Commissioner the same salary as for the Recorder of London, and for the other Commissioners the same as that for the Common Serjeant.[19]

A Commissioner for Great Britain has no jurisdiction in Northern Ireland, which has its own very similar but not identical system and its own Commissioners including a Chief Commissioner.[20]

The powers of the Chief Commissioner actually conferred by statute differ from those of the other Commissioners only in that the former alone has power to order an appeal or application to be dealt with by a tribunal of three Commissioners.[21] In matters of adjudication each Commissioner is of course solely responsible for his own decisions, and the Chief Commissioner has no power to give general directions relating to adjudication or to intervene in any way in an appeal being dealt with by another Commissioner. Some members of the public believe that the Chief Commissioner has power to reverse a decision of another Commissioner. He has no such power. In matters of administration, however, the difference is very great. The Chief Commissioner decides which decisions of the Commissioners shall be reported,[22] though he consults the other Commissioners on this and many other administrative matters both from day to day and at the periodical conferences of all the Commissioners. In the last resort he decides all internal administrative matters relating to the three offices in London, Edinburgh and Cardiff and also speaks for the whole body of Commissioners in external matters. He is sometimes referred to as the President of the national insurance tribunals of Great Britain, but in fact he has no general statutory presidential powers. The practical difference between his position in matters of administration and that of the other Commissioners depends largely on accepted custom.

A Commissioner's powers and duties as a tribunal depend not only on the very general indications of them in the Acts and regulations but also on the nature of the questions entrusted to him for decision and the generally accepted understanding of the differences between courts and tribunals. This gives the Commissioners in matters of procedure a considerable opportunity for the exercise, according to law, of individual judgment and indeed improvisation in the light of the special circumstances of claimants. These opportunities my predecessor Sir David Davies and those who worked with him seized with both hands, and we who came after tried to do the same.

Notes

[1] As to the meaning of the phrases "the Commissioner" and "a Commissioner," see the N.I. Act 1966, s. 9, and p. 13. above.

[2] See ss. 116 and 168 (1) and Sched. 20.

[3] For the corresponding earlier provisions, see the N.I. Act 1966, s. 9, the 1965 Act, s. 78 and the 1946 Act, s. 43 (3) (*c*). There were similar provisions in the Industrial Injuries Acts. In the recent publication referred to in note 50 on p. 146, Professor Calvert criticizes this qualification and proposes a different career structure with an adjudication structure covering supplementary benefit as well as the subject-matter of my lectures.

[4] I possess four such appointments, two dated Jan. 1, 1959, as a deputy Commissioner, two dated May 10, 1961, as the Commissioner. I have none as Chief Commissioner, since I was deemed to have been appointed to that office by section 9 of the 1966 Act.

[5] Statements in some earlier editions of text-books that Commissioners are appointed by the Minister have never been correct.

[6] See the 1975 Act, Sched. 10, para. 4.

[7] Under Sched. 10, para. 5. A Commissioner's pension comes within the Administration of Justice (Pensions) Act 1950 and regulations under the Administration of Justice Act 1973, with the result that a gratuity is payable, the amount of which may depend on an election by the Commissioner under regulations under the latter Act. It also comes within the Pensions (Increase) Act 1971, s. 2 of which provides for indexing.

[8] The offices of the National Insurance Commissioner and the Industrial Injuries Commissioner were held by His Honour Sir David Davies Q.C. (formerly a county court judge) from before 1948 to May 1961 and by myself from 1961 to 1966, when by virtue of s. 9 I automatically became the Chief Commissioner. I held that office until May 1975, when Mr. Temple succeeded me. The present Commissioners

in order of seniority are: Mr. H. A. Shewan Q.C. (Edinburgh) 1955–; Mr. D. W. E. Neligan (formerly part-time) 1961–; Mr. D. Reith Q.C. (Edinburgh) (formerly part-time) 1964–; Mr. H. B. Magnus Q.C. 1964–; Mr. J. S. Watson Q.C. 1965–; Mr. R. S. Lazarus Q.C. 1966–; Mr. E. R. Bowen Q.C. (Cardiff) 1967–; and Mr. J. G. Monroe 1973–. Others who held office for long periods were: Sir Archibald Safford Q.C. 1948–61, Mr. N. P. d'Albuquerque 1948–66, Mr. A. P. Duffes Q.C. (Edinburgh) 1948–54, Mr. G. Owen George (Cardiff) 1950–67 and Mr. H. I. Nelson Q.C. 1959–69; and for shorter periods His Honour G. Clark Williams K.C. (formerly Judge Clark Williams); Mr. R. G. Clover Q.C. (now His Honour Judge Clover Q.C.); Sir Ronald Morison Q.C. (Edinburgh); Mr. J. J. H. Barrington (later His Honour Judge Barrington); Mr. G. Granville Slack (now His Honour Judge Granville Slack) and Mr. M. O'C. Stranders Q.C. who unhappily died not long after his appointment as a full-time Commissioner. The Umpire over a long period was Sir Ernest W. Wingate-Saul K.C.

[9] See particularly the Tribunals and Inquiries Act 1971, ss. 1 (1) (*a*) and 19 (3) and Sched. 1, para. 18, replacing similar provisions in the Tribunals and Inquiries Act 1958; and para. 30A inserted by the Consequential Provisions Act, Sched. 2, para. 46.

[10] He cannot except on appeal review his own decisions.

[11] The 1975 Act, ss. 101, 112 and 106 (2) and the S.S. Pensions Act 1975 and the Mobility Allowance regs. 1975 [S.I. 1975 No. 1573], Pt. IV. See also n. 12 on p. 19 as to certain other questions which are or were for decision by a Commissioner.

[12] [1962] 2 Q.B. 677 at p. 685.

[13] I.I. Acts 1946, s. 51 (5) and 1965, s. 50 (6).

[14] N.I. (I.I.) (D.C.Q.) (No. 2) regs. 1967 [S.I. 1967 No. 1571], reg. 1 (2).

[15] 1975 Act, s. 97, marginal note. This section provides for the appointment of insurance officers, local tribunals and Commissioners. There was therefore an opportunity of introducing positively into statute law the phrase "the statutory authorities." The opportunity was not taken. As to that phrase, see further n. 4 on p. 18.

[16] S.S. (Claims and Payments) regs. 1975 [S.I. 1975 No. 560], reg. 2 (1).

[17] 1975 Act, s. 115 (2), for the purposes of Sched. 13, and the S.S. (D.C.Q.) regs. 1975 [S.I. 1975 No. 558], reg. 2 (1).

[18] There are other specialist medical authorities for certain purposes in prescribed disease cases; see the S.S. (I.I.) (P.D.) regs. 1975 [S.I. 1975 No. 1537], Pts. V and VI.

[19] See the Report on Top Salaries (Chairman Lord Boyle of Handsworth) Cmnd. 5846, Chap. 7, esp. paras. 94 and 150. The annual amounts recommended were £15,500 and £14,000 respectively as from Jan. 1, 1975, but only parts of the increases were paid from that date.

[20] Mr. T. A. Blair Q.C.

[21] See the 1975 Act, s. 116.

[22] See p. 78, n. 12.

Chapter Six

APPEAL TO A COMMISSIONER

Appeal to a Commissioner

It is often said that national insurance and social security proceedings are and should be conducted informally and that they are more in the nature of an inquiry than a contest between parties. On the other hand there is the weighty opinion of the Franks Committee that informality without rules of procedure may be positively inimical to right adjudication.[1] The word " informal " when used in relation to legal proceedings is a relative term. Informality may be present in different types of proceedings to different extents. It is unnecessary to consider whether there are some types which are absolutely formal. Proceedings before a Commissioner certainly are not that. In them, however, every appellant is required by statute [2] to state his grounds of appeal in writing. A hearing is normally in public.[3] Regulations give a right to call witnesses and to put questions directly to any witnesses called at a hearing.[4] These facts alone call for a certain degree of formality and order.

Informality may result from either or both of two causes. It may be unintended, having crept into the proceedings because the tribunal or others are not sufficiently aware of the need for some formality. It may also be part of a deliberate policy. It is important not only that the Commissioner should give the correct decision but also that all should have had a full opportunity of expressing their points of view and should be able to see, whether the claim succeeds or fails, that it has been considered fully and fairly. If informality is deliberately practised to achieve these or other proper purposes then it is justified and desirable: the Franks Committee commended " the combination of a formal procedure with an informal atmosphere." I hope that what follows will show that the Commissioners are not merely seeking to achieve this but succeeding in doing so.

If one compares the rules laid down by and under statutes

for the conduct of court proceedings with those governing the procedure of Commissioners one must be struck by the extraordinary scantiness of the latter. There is no provision for cross-appeals, nor for anything in the nature of pleadings or particulars or interlocutory proceedings except requests for oral hearings. There is no provision for discovery of documents. The rules governing the admissibility of evidence do not apply. There has always been in the regulations a provision having the effect that subject to the provisions of the Act and regulations the procedure shall be such as the Commissioner determines.[5] This creates extensive opportunities for the exercise of improvisation by the Commissioners, of course within the scope of such rules as there are and the rules of natural justice, and taking into account the special needs of those concerned.

Most claimants are unrepresented. If one reads the statistics of illiteracy one must assume that some of them cannot read or write, though I do not recall any claimant ever telling me in terms that he could not: it is a subject on which those concerned are reserved. But often it has been possible reading between the lines to tell that that is the situation. Many other claimants though not illiterate are not highly educated, and few of them or their representatives are familiar with the complexities of this branch of the law. These facts exert a powerful influence on the type of procedure that is most appropriate. Many of the gaps have been filled by the admirable Form L.T.2 [6] put before the local tribunal and the insurance officer's further submission to the Commissioner.

In this lecture I propose to describe some of the incidents of an appeal to a Commissioner in the minority of cases where a hearing is held.

The commonest type of case is an appeal by an unrepresented claimant against a decision of a local tribunal.[7]

The claimant has three months within which to appeal to a Commissioner from a local tribunal.[8] He does so by completing a very simple form provided by the Department. In it strictly speaking he must state his grounds of appeal,[8] but in practice the Commissioners always construe such grounds submitted by claimants with the utmost liberality, and there have been a number of cases where the insurance officer has raised a point in favour of a claimant that was not in his grounds of appeal at all; sometimes a Commissioner has done the same, though giving the insurance officer an opportunity of dealing with the matter.[9] There have indeed been cases where in the interests of the claimant the insurance officer has appealed against a local tribunal's decision disallowing the claim. The appeal form has to be sent as required by the statute to a local office of the Department,[10] from which it is forwarded to the quite separate office of the Chief Insurance Officer situated formerly in London but now in Southampton. At the same time notification is sent to the Commissioners' office, so that if a substantial time elapses and nothing has happened that office can make inquiries. In due course the insurance officer who has now taken over the case from the local insurance officer delivers a written submission with the other papers to the Commissioners' office. Identical copies are sent to the claimant. The papers include the form L.T.2 which was before the local tribunal. On receipt of the insurance officer's submission to the Commissioner and the other papers the claimant is given an opportunity of submitting further evidence and observations, and at this stage he is asked whether he requests an oral hearing.[11] If he requests a hearing the Commissioner dealing with the case decides whether it is to be granted. This like any other interlocutory question is decided by a Commissioner himself.

Hearing by a Commissioner

Hearings by Commissioners are held in London, Edinburgh and Cardiff. Subject to this, the procedure is designed to meet the claimant's convenience so far as possible. Here the fact that each Commissioner has jurisdiction throughout Great Britain is most useful. The claimant's wishes as to the place of the hearing are taken into account, and cases from the western counties of England are often heard in Cardiff and from the northern counties in Edinburgh; the hearing takes place in whichever of the three places is most convenient to the claimant or his representative.[12] The fact that the majority of appeals to Commissioners are decided on the papers without a hearing has a most beneficial side effect. A Commissioner need never put a number of cases in his list for fear that some unexpected development may leave him without work to do. There is always work to be done in his room. This enables a date and time to be fixed for every hearing, and even when we were under the heaviest pressure we were always able to adhere to this. The advantage to all concerned need not be emphasised.

In addition to being notified well in advance of the time and place of the hearing the claimant is sent papers explaining the expenses allowed and the method by which he can before the hearing obtain a voucher which he can exchange for a railway ticket. An unusual feature of the procedure is that before a hearing in London he is sent a sketch plan of the immediate neighbourhood of the Commissioners' London office to help him to get there.

On arrival the claimant will be met by someone experienced in helping claimants, who is familiar with their problems, difficulties, anxieties and wishes.

The court room at Grosvenor Gardens though small fulfils its purpose admirably in every way.[13] As in many rooms where tribunals sit there is no bench or dais. The main furniture consists of two long tables placed parallel to each other. The Commissioner sits in the middle of one, with the legal assistant acting as clerk of the court at the end of it taking a note and being ready to help in any way necessary. (There is nobody present to perform the duties of an usher.) The insurance officer and the claimant sit at the other table facing the Commissioner both at an equal distance from him; the claimant cannot reasonably feel that the insurance officer is occupying a more favourable position than he or " has the ear of the Court." I attach great importance to this type of layout for this sort of proceeding as being least likely to overawe the claimant and thereby inhibit him from presenting his case fully. The arrangements have also the great advantage of flexibility. In a case [14] not long before my retirement the claimant was extremely deaf. This presented no problem. He came and sat at the end of my table. I moved my chair down to the left of him. The insurance officer at my invitation sat opposite me. The claimant's representative sat between them. Seated thus, we all managed to hear each other.

Some claimants have before the hearing expressed concern because it was to be in public. If a claim is a genuine one there is no cause for alarm. The courtroom is more of a room than a court. Members of the public only very rarely attend. I have always found the representatives of the Press Association and the Press most helpful and considerate, and I cannot remember any complaint after a hearing of an unfair press report or comment, and many claimants have at the end of a hearing indicated that their concern had been unfounded.

At the beginning of the hearing there is a little formality. When everyone is assembled the Commissioner comes into the courtroom preceded by a messenger, who knocks on the door and calls on everyone in court to stand for the Commissioner. (Special arrangements are made if anyone is disabled.) I think that this amount of formality is desirable. It marks the fact that the hearing is starting. It identifies the Commissioner for the claimant.[15] Moreover I think that it would be undignified for the Commissioner to come in unannounced, and probably embarrassing to others sitting about and talking when they realised that he had come in.

At a hearing neither the Commissioner nor anyone else is in legal robes. As to other clothing I never concerned myself with that. I always assumed that people would be decently dressed, and they always were, even if their dress was sometimes unusual. One man wore his cap throughout a hearing: if he was hoping for some reaction from me he must have been disappointed, for I took no notice. Once many years ago I gave a ruling on a woman's clothing, but I understand that what I said was not well received in Scotland and I have relegated the story to the comparative obscurity of a footnote.[16]

Anyone is permitted to address the Commissioner or give evidence either standing or sitting as he prefers. In practice the whole proceedings are conducted with everyone seated.

This brings us to the moment when the hearing begins. In

the courts in London the judge needs to say no more to counsel, whose duty it is to open the case than "Yes, Mr. So and So," and that is the recognised signal for counsel to begin. Before a tribunal the situation is completely different. An unrepresented claimant may feel alone in unfamiliar territory. His ideas on what happens in courts may have been derived from television or possibly from one of the many departmental leaflets which describe the Commissioner as "of high legal standing and appointed by the Crown." Especially if he is elderly, he may be unaccustomed to addressing someone "of high legal standing" in public without a clear invitation to do so. On the other hand he probably is most anxious to state his case in his own way, and the Commissioner must be wanting to hear it since he has granted or directed an oral hearing. But—and I have often seen this happen—at the critical moment the claimant's thoughts may all scatter, and he may find himself incapable of thinking or saying anything and may become helplessly confused. The problem is how the Commissioner should best, whilst maintaining judicial independence, help the claimant to say what he wants to say, whatever that may be, and establish a mutual understanding between them. Here, I think, two principles are equally important.

First, the claimant must if necessary be positively encouraged to speak, and it may be necessary to repeat the invitation, perhaps more than once. Obviously there are many ways for the tribunal to do this; one is to draw his attention to the main point which *he* relied on in his grounds of appeal, and ask whether he wants to say anything about that. Secondly, he must be allowed at the start to put his case in his own way. In some appeals from local tribunals and medical appeal tribunals with which I have dealt, and the other Commissioners must have dealt with others, the first complaint in the grounds of appeal has been: "I did not get a fair hearing. I was never allowed to put my case in my own way." If at the outset the tribunal or chairman tells the claimant that there is only one point in the case, which is so and so, and will he please deal with that, the claimant may simply dry up, and almost certainly he will go away feeling that he has not had a fair hearing, to which after all he had a statutory right. He should therefore be allowed for a time to go on in his own way so as not to interrupt his train of thought; but if after a time it becomes clear that what he is saying is totally irrelevant, then—but only after a time—he should be brought round delicately to the point in the case.

If the insurance officer calls a witness on a disputed matter this may create a serious problem. My experience has been that most claimants, many representatives and indeed some insurance officers have no idea how to cross-examine effectively. I have been surprised at the number of cases where a witness has not been asked even the elementary question why in a signed statement he said the exact opposite of what he is saying now. A case where firm cross-examination is desirable poses serious problems. If the claimant does not cross-examine the witness at all the insurance officer cannot strictly speaking re-examine so as to elucidate matters; and in any event he can hardly be expected to attempt to demolish the evidence of the witness whom he has called. If no one cross-examines the witness there may be two conflicting stories with little means of telling which is to be preferred. If the Commissioner questions the witness there is the danger that he may appear to be taking sides. In some cases however this may be the lesser evil.

Though there is no rule saying so, in practice whoever has opened the proceedings is always given the last word. This is one instance of many where Commissioners and tribunal chairmen follow procedures which are instinctive as a result of their practice in other branches of the law.

When the claimant is represented further problems may arise. Two occur frequently.

The distinction between a representative and a witness is frequently confused. In many cases a representative, especially a trade union representative, has given me verbally a statement of facts and then intimated that he did not intend to call as a witness the claimant, who was present, to substantiate his statements. Such a procedure is based on a complete misunderstanding of the function of a representative. In that capacity he is not a witness any more than the insurance officer is. His statements, if evidence at all, are hearsay, of far less weight than direct evidence which can be tested by cross-examination. Where the representative makes a statement and does not call the evidence to substantiate it this completely stultifies the regulation which entitles everyone including the insurance officer to question any witness called.[17] A representative's function is to argue questions of law and comment on the facts which have been or will be proved by evidence. Where those facts are proved by a number of different items of evidence it may be helpful for him to state them in a clear, logical order. Where the only evidence is that of the claimant it may be better for him to call the claimant straight away so as not even to give the impression of putting words into his mouth.

Legal Aid

Reference to representation by lawyers and others naturally leads on to the question of legal aid, on which I shall now digress. It has never been available in any of the following five proceedings: the consideration of an appeal (in which expressions throughout this discussion I include an application) to a Commissioner from a medical appeal tribunal, or from the Attendance Allowance Board, or from a local tribunal; nor at a hearing by a medical appeal tribunal or a local tribunal. The introduction of legal advice and assistance in 1972 [18] and the extensive use that can be made of these facilities as shown by the decision of the Court of Appeal in *McKenzie* v. *McKenzie* in 1971 [19] in my opinion radically alter the situation. A lawyer can, in addition to helping the claimant with the preparation of his claim or appeal, accompany him to a hearing of any of the above five types of proceeding and give him advice and suggestions at the hearing, though he may not actually take part by addressing the tribunal or examining witnesses. In 1973 a Tribunal of Commissioners encouraged the use of these facilities,[20] but down to the date of my retirement I had the impression that, though some legal publications had noted our remarks, much less use was being made of them than might have been. Moreover it can be argued that a considerable amount of help is already given to claimants in different forms by officers of the Departments, and that with the legal advice and assistance now available the claimant has something so near to that which legal aid would give him that in an imperfect world and the financial state of this country more cannot reasonably be asked for. My own view, however, is that in a very small proportion of the cases there is a gap which only legal aid can fill, and that the objective should be to provide it for these few cases, with stringent restrictions to exclude it from the vast majority of cases where it is unnecessary and could be undesirable.

In October 1973 the Lord Chancellor's Legal Aid Advisory Committee recommended the extension of legal aid to all tribunals within the classes described by them, which included Commissioners and medical appeal and local tribunals.[21] The Committee did not suggest any order of priority as between tribunals in the different classes considering that such an approach would be unsound.[21]

I respectfully support the recommendation of the Advisory Committee in respect of all the five types of proceeding, though in view of the special position of national insurance tribunals I submit that the machinery should be different from that contained in their general recommendation. Moreover, since it seems probable that financial considerations will make it impossible at present to make legal aid available for all five types of proceeding I am recording my view as to the priorities between them.

Hearings by a Commissioner of an appeal from a medical appeal tribunal. I think that this class of case should be given the highest priority. The numbers are comparatively small.[22] Many applications and appeals are dealt with together, and my impression is that an oral hearing is held in only a small proportion of these cases. Many claimants are not able to detect or even understand a point of law. The law governing the making of assessments is complex. The amount at stake may be very considerable. Vigilance is necessary to ensure that the rules of natural justice are not contravened even inadvertently.

Hearing by a Commissioner of an appeal from the Attendance Allowance Board. Here the figures are smaller still.[23] I think that similar considerations apply. The amount at stake is likely to be smaller, but since no hearing is held by the board even greater vigilance is necessary.

Hearing by a Commissioner of an appeal from a local tribunal. Here the number of appeals is much larger.[24] As there is a right to call evidence before the Commissioner which was not called before the local tribunal and to cross-examine witnesses, this may be the only opportunity of cross-examining an important witness. The amount at stake may be very large.[25] The Commissioner's decision is final on questions of fact. I think that here there is a need for legal aid in a very small proportion of cases (mostly industrial injuries ones), though the cost would be considerably greater than in the other types of appeal which I have discussed.

Hearing by a medical appeal tribunal. Here the figures are much larger: 13,000 appeals in 1974. If legal aid were made available and advantage were taken of it on a substantial scale, it might be necessary to obtain a substantial number of additional members of tribunals as well as lawyers competent to act as representatives of the claimants, which might pose serious problems. Nevertheless the tribunal's decision on the facts is final, and here again the amount at stake may be very large.[25]

Hearing by a local tribunal. I think that this type of proceeding should have the lowest priority. Here the practical problems are even more formidable, the figures being double those for medical appeal tribunals.[26] The case is not so strong since the local tribunal's findings of fact are not final; there is an appeal on fact as well as law to a Commissioner. Nevertheless the hearing locally by the local tribunal may be the only occasion when witnesses are willing to attend, and therefore the only practical opportunity of questioning them.

Conclusion on legal aid. On the whole I think that legal aid ought to be made available at each of the five types of tribunal,[27] the order of priority being that in which I have discussed them. Provision of it should be subject to very stringent conditions designed to ensure that it would be granted only in a very small minority of cases where it is really needed, and should not be granted as a matter of course where it is not. I share the view of the Council on Tribunals that the test in national insurance cases should be more restricted than that in section 7 (5) of the Legal Aid Act 1974.[28] Moreover I think it essential that the grant or refusal of legal aid should be made, not by the normal method, but by a Commissioner or chairman of the tribunal concerned, who should have power to refuse legal aid but grant legal advice and assistance or if appropriate extend the financial limit, if that was all that was necessary, as an alternative to granting legal aid. They would be far better equipped than anyone else to discriminate between cases and decide whether legal aid was necessary. It would probably be necessary to give further consideration to the whole question of costs, expenses and contributions in national insurance proceedings, since many claimants regard themselves as being engaged in a dispute with a body which they cannot distinguish from the one which assesses a claimant's means under the legal aid scheme.

From experience of appeals where the claimant has been represented by a lawyer I do not think that the provision of legal aid need necessarily damage the atmosphere of the proceedings. Nor do I agree with the argument sometimes advanced that the tribunal can perfectly well look after the claimant's interests. An independent tribunal cannot advise a claimant in advance what evidence to adduce.

My hope therefore is that legal aid will be introduced as soon as possible; if this hope is shared by others it makes it all the more urgent that legal education and training should help to equip those entering the legal profession to play a part in national insurance work.

Assistance and representation by lay organisation. On the question of help from lay organisations and persons other than lawyers I am in complete agreement with paragraphs 33 and 34 of the Committee's Report.[29] I think that there is a need for a great expansion of the work of such organisations and persons, some of whom are mentioned in those paragraphs and in appendix D to the Report. I agree with the Committee as to the method of achieving the expansion. I should expect that the help would be most useful in the earliest stages in alerting persons who otherwise might not claim at all, preparing coherent written statements from them, helping them if necessary to obtain advice from the Department and if necessary showing them how to set about obtaining legal advice or assistance. At the Commissioner level their services could be of value depending on the amount that they were able and willing to put into the work. At the least they might help the claimant merely by accompanying him to a hearing, giving him moral support and giving him such help as he might need due, for example, to incapacity, language difficulties and so on. But a lay representative may be able to do much more than this, as is shown by many insurance officers and some union representatives. Insurance officers never or hardly ever have had any formal legal training. Nevertheless as the result of long experience of handling cases, attending hearings and study of the relevant legislation and of decisions and other materials explaining it they often achieve a quite outstanding expertise, as their written submissions and their presentation of cases at hearings clearly show. If lay representatives in organisations are prepared to apply themselves similarly to national insurance law, or to some specific part of it, as the specialist insurance officers do, their services could be of outstanding value to claimants. The word "specialist" may give a pointer to a solution. It might well be possible for a layman who specialised in one particular type of benefit to obtain a sufficient mastery of the law relating to that to enable him to give real help to claimants who might be in special need of it.[30]

Compelling the Attendance of Witnesses

The 1975 Act, like the earlier Acts, enables regulations to provide for compelling witnesses to attend and give evidence.[31] The power has been exercised in relation to certain other inquiries,[32] but never in relation to the statutory authorities, and some people have asked why. I think that where a power has existed for some 30 years and has never been exercised one can reasonably start with the assumption that those concerned must have thought that there were good reasons for not exercising it.[33] These however would be recorded in the archives of the Department, and I can only surmise what they may have been. Cases where the absence of first hand evidence has made me feel doubtful whether, if there had been more evidence, I might have come to a different decision have most commonly been appeals relating to disqualification for misconduct under what is now section 20 of the 1975 Act: for example where a claimant told a story which I strongly suspected to be a cock-and-bull story but the employers, no doubt for reasons which they thought compelling on industrial relations or commercial grounds, had supplied little or no worthwhile information. The Commissioners have laid down that in all cases concerning misconduct those who allege it must prove it by satisfactory evidence.[34] It may be that in such cases some claimants who should have incurred disqualification escaped it. Other cases are where a claimant wants a witness brought in order to cross-examine him. In many cases the insurance officer obliges and produces the witness voluntarily. In those cases where the efforts of the claimant or his representative and the insurance officer are ineffective it seems to me highly doubtful how valuable compulsion would be. Every advocate knows how difficult it is to get anything out of a hostile witness. Some requests for the attendance of a witness are plainly irresponsible or absurd. It would therefore be necessary in any regulations to provide for someone to decide whether the witness should be compelled to attend or not. It is difficult to see who the prescribed person would be. In many cases only someone who had read the whole of the other evidence could judge whether the attendance of the witness was necessary. There is no one available to a Commissioner similar to a Master or Registrar. If the Commissioner decided it himself the claimant would probably think if the decision were adverse that he had already made up his mind or was taking sides. The same would happen if the decision were entrusted to the Department or the insurance officer. Questions of cost and expenses are also relevant. The claimant's expenses of attending a hearing are paid according to a scale, and presumably the regulations would have to provide for something in the nature of conduct money for witnesses. Who would pay this? In many proceedings there is a sanction against the unnecessary attendance of witnesses in the form of awards of or disallowances of costs. In proceedings before a Commissioner costs are not awarded against anyone. In respect of these matters the regulation might place the insurance officer, who has access to funds, at a great advantage over most claimants.

The strict rules as to the admissibility of evidence do not apply in these proceedings, and signed statements and even hearsay evidence of witnesses who do not attend are frequently acted on. If a witness has refused to give a statement or to attend, it is problematical whether he will say anything which will be relevant. It is important that the procedure before Commissioners as well as local tribunals should be kept as uncomplicated as possible, even if in some cases this may result in rough justice. Morever in the last resort there may be other ways of compelling a witness to attend.[35] Balancing the advantages against the disadvantages, I incline to the view that a succession of Ministers and Secretaries of State have been wise to refrain from exercising this power. Others may however think differently. At the first Edinburgh Conference of local tribunal members I expressed some such view, thereby bringing on my head later a charge of complacency.[36]

Evidence on Oath

At a hearing before a Commissioner evidence is in practice given not on oath, and written evidence is not by affidavit. The question has occasionally been raised whether the Commissioner has power or even a duty to administer an oath. The position seems to be different in England and Scotland. The statutes have always contained in relation to different adjudicating authorities either a provision permitting an oath to be administered or one enabling regulations to permit it.[37] It seems that for England such a power was unnecessary in respect of the statutory authorities because any tribunal can administer an oath under the Evidence Act 1851, s. 16.[37] That Act however does not apply to Scotland, and I must leave it to others to discuss whether the position is the same in

Scotland though for different reasons and if not whether any change is desirable.[38]

Medical Assessors

A difficult problem to which I think that no completely satisfactory solution has yet been found concerns the use by the Commissioners of the services of medical assessors. There has been power to use them in industrial injuries cases since 1948 and in national insurance cases since 1955, at first under regulations and now under the Act itself.[39] The practice of different Commissioners has varied. One used them extensively in industrial injuries cases; another used them hardly ever, if at all. A Commissioner can usually ascertain the meaning of medical expressions from amongst other things medical dictionaries. The most valuable help which an assessor can give is on causation: for example whether it is accepted in the medical profession by those best qualified to judge that A causes or contributes to causing B always, or frequently, or sometimes, or infrequently, or never; and what other factors affect the answer to such questions, and how. The judgment of the Divisional Court in the *Jones* case (1962) was helpful in that by implication at least it approved of resort to medical dictionaries as opposed to general ones.[40] But in that case the Court quashed the Commissioner's decision not only because he had not informed the parties that after the hearing he had consulted a medical assessor and had not given them an opportunity of commenting or calling further evidence, but also because the medical assessor's answers to three questions, set out in the Lord Chief Justice's judgment, which were all questions of causation, " quite clearly exceeded the functions of an assessor . . . ," the function of an assessor being not to supply evidence but to help the tribunal to weigh the evidence given by others.[41] The effect of this decision therefore was that the advice of a medical assessor is unavailable where it is most likely to be useful. If event B follows immediately after A the claimant may produce no medical evidence but may simply argue that it is an impossible coincidence if A had nothing to do with B. In such a case the services of a medical assessor could be of the greatest value if he were allowed to express an opinion on causation. The alternative procedure held by the Court to be proper of referring questions for examination and report[42] is likely to be far more cumbersome. The form of the questions may depend on the exact findings of fact of the Commissioner. If for that or other reasons the reference is delayed until after the hearing there can for many reasons be further delay, especially as all concerned must be given an opportunity to comment on the report and each other's comments. If the reference is before the hearing it may involve framing and answering numerous alternative questions, many of which in the event may not arise. If a decision is to be reached by the Commissioner which is both medically well informed and quick, there seems to be much to be said for the view that it should be open to the Commissioner, after he and the assessor have heard all the evidence and read all the papers, to retire with the assessor, tell him his findings of fact and ask him taking fully into account any opinions expressed in the evidence what is his view of the probabilities on causation. This course goes far beyond what the *Jones* case shows to be permissible. My recollection though I cannot confirm it by statistics is that after the *Jones* case there was a marked falling off in the use of medical assessors by Commissioners. I think that there is a real problem here which deserves consideration in depth, after which there might well be found to be a good case for exercising the power of extending the functions of assessors.[43] The opportunity might be taken of clearing up certain uncertainties in this field. I have gained the impression that there are considerable differences in practice at local tribunal level as to the use made of assessors and the procedure in connection with them. The House of Lords in a case under the Workmen's Compensation Acts decided that where the assessor's advice was likely to affect the result the party should be informed of it; and that it was not part of a medical assessor's function to examine the workman personally.[44] I do not know whether both these rulings are applied consistently.

Medical Evidence

In this situation the Commissioners have been greatly helped by the practice whereby in many cases, especially industrial injuries ones involving medical questions, the insurance officer has obtained a written statement of medical evidence from a senior medical officer (occasionally a principal medical officer) of the Department. The statement is included in the evidence and if a hearing is held the medical officer is called as a witness. Such witnesses are sometimes attacked by or on behalf of claimants on the ground that they are salaried officers of the Department, as they clearly are: and that they always advise against the claimant, which they clearly do not. An impartial observer at a succession of hearings, such as a press representative, might get that impression. But in fact in many cases the statement of the medical officer supports the claimant's case, whereupon the insurance officer takes appropriate steps according to the state of the proceedings to ensure if he can that the claim succeeds. The public probably hears nothing of this, and there is therefore a real danger of a wrong impression being created. My own impression over many years is that the medical officers of the Department in the evidence which they have given before me have maintained a very high standard of responsibility and a most commendably dispassionate approach to the problems on which they have given evidence. Two particularly helpful features in their evidence I have noticed. Sometimes they express their opinion in an alternative form: *e.g.* if the description of the accident given in document X is accepted, my opinion would be this; if that in document Y, it would be that. On a number of occasions before me a somewhat different account of the accident has emerged at the hearing, whereupon the insurance officer has told me that the medical officer wishes me to know that if that account is accepted his evidence would be favourable to the claimant. Secondly the practice of referring to standard medical works in support of an opinion is most helpful. Where one is given two flatly contradictory opinions as to causation or other matters it is extremely helpful to know what well-known medical writers say.

Nevertheless the approaches of a doctor and a lawyer to the same problem are frequently very different, as two examples will show. The first concerns standard of proof. A doctor trained in medical science is usually not prepared to say that A is B unless this has been proved to be true beyond any possibility of doubt. A tribunal must accept a much less exacting standard. Usually the question for its decision is whether it is more probable than not that A is B, assuming this to be a matter of reasonable inference and not merely guessing. In a case therefore where a doctor says that it is not proved that A is B it does not necessarily follow that a tribunal will say the same. A second difference concerns the ascertainment of the facts. Lawyers throughout their training and experience are saturated with ideas of natural justice, including the belief that in all legal proceedings a person is entitled to know who is giving evidence affecting his interests, and what that evidence is, so that he may have a chance of challenging it. This instinct is much less ingrained in many doctors, and where the decision of or an opinion on any question is entrusted to doctors continuous vigilance is necessary to ensure that they are not acting on secret instructions supplied to them from behind the scenes. If anyone thinks that this fear is fanciful let him read paragraphs 13 and 14 of Decision C.I. 43/67 (not reported). In that case the issue was whether a man's death had resulted from the lung condition known as pneumoconiosis. That question was for *decision* by the statutory authorities and not by a pneumoconiosis medical board, but, as is customary in such cases, an *opinion* of a pneumoconiosis medical panel was put in evidence; but it was no more than an opinion. At the hearing counsel for the claimant by cross-examination elicited the fact that a document existed entitled " In Confidence—Pneumoconiosis Medical Panels—Standards to be applied in deciding pneumoconiosis death claims—S.M.O. (Pn) Conference, August, 1966." The document laid down certain tests, some based on measurements, for deciding whether pneumoconiosis " would " or " will " be considered to have played a part in causing death. This was the first time that any Commissioner had ever heard of such a document, and in paragraph

14 of the decision I commented on it. It could of course result in a panel's expressing the view that pneumoconiosis was insufficient to cause death because of certain measurements, when they thought that in fact it could have done so. It is my emphatic opinion that *all* the materials on which adjudication in any form by anyone is based should be available to the claimant.

The following matter may be closely related. The duty of deciding whether a person is suffering from pneumoconiosis has always been entrusted by the statutory regulations to a pneumoconiosis medical board, against whose decision there has never been a right of appeal to a medical appeal tribunal.[45] For many years a discreet little statement has appeared in the Department's Annual Reports that "The central pneumoconiosis medical panel continues to give further consideration to certain particularly difficult diagnosis cases."[46] I do not remember any Commissioner's decision in which the work of this central panel has been discussed, and it is improbable that it would be since the Commissioners have no jurisdiction to decide diagnosis questions.[47] In December 1975 it was announced that this system "was less satisfactory than a formal right of appeal would be" and it was now "to be replaced by a statutory right of appeal on diagnosis" to a (specially qualified) medical appeal tribunal.[48] If this announcement means what it seems to mean, the proposed change would seem to be a most desirable one.

I should like to refer to a particularly commendable practice followed by certain trade unions. Sometimes a member of a union does not consult them until the time for appealing to a Commissioner has nearly expired but there is a medical issue on which the union wish to obtain a specialist's opinion, which often takes time. The union that I have particularly in mind submit a formal notice of appeal to prevent the time from expiring, stating that as soon as a medical report has been obtained it will be submitted. In due course this is done, whether the report is favourable to the claimant's case or not. If it is, it is relied on as the grounds of appeal; if it is not, the appeal may be abandoned. This practice designed to help in the ascertainment of the truth whatever it may be seems to me a very proper one and to contrast very favourably with the procedure adopted in some other branches of the law.[49]

I have stressed earlier the desirability of an early understanding between the claimant and the Commissioner at a hearing. This may be important for an additional reason. Sometimes there is a section or regulation which makes it impossible for the claim to succeed; but the claimant seems unable either by reading the papers or listening to the insurance officer to believe that the situation is as the latter has described it. In such a case it may be helpful for the claimant, with guidance from the Commissioner, to look at the actual Act or regulation.[50] In a number of cases the claimant has at last by some such means been helped at least to understand the true situation, even if he is not pleased with it. But this can only be achieved if an understanding has already been built up between the claimant and the Commissioner.

At the end of the hearing there is hardly ever any discussion about costs. The expenses of the claimant and any witnesses properly called and of a companion if the claimant is genuinely incapable of travelling alone are paid in accordance with a scale irrespective of the result of the appeal. Costs of legal or trade union representatives are not paid. This system may be more favourable to those who lose and less favourable to those who win than the system prevailing in some other jurisdictions where costs follow the event. But in one way the system is outstandingly favourable to every claimant. He knows in advance precisely how he stands in relation to costs: he does not run the risk, having won before the tribunal, of losing an appeal and thereby incurring heavy costs. I consider this to be a point of overwhelming importance.

From time to time complaints are received that the scales of expenses are so low as to make it in some cases impossible for the claimant to call medical evidence which he has been advised to call. This is a serious and, I think, a difficult matter. It is not easy to think of a method by which the payment of exceptional expenses could be confined to the few cases where it is really justified. It is particularly important that, unless and until the scale is made more flexible, the medical officers of the department should continue to maintain the dispassionate attitude towards cases that they do at present.

I should like to conclude this chapter with a reference to the very valuable work done in this field by the insurance officers. An insurance officer is a civil servant. In most cases he works in the local office of the Department of Health and Social Security,[51] part of the time as an officer of that Department, and for the rest as an insurance officer, in respect of which work he comes under the Chief Insurance Officer's office which is separate from the offices of the Department. As an insurance officer he performs two distinct duties: deciding claims or questions and submitting cases to local tribunals and Commissioners. I have seen a lot of the work of insurance officers and formed the highest opinion of it. In giving their decisions they are acting administratively,[52] but they do not act, as some claimants assert, as " rubber stamps " for or on secret instructions from the Department; like the other statutory authorities they apply the relevant legislation and case law. In submitting cases their purpose—and in this they have the active encouragement of the Commissioners—is to ensure, so far as is in their power, not only that the claimant does not receive more than he is entitled to, but also that he does not receive less. Effect is given by the insurance officers to this purpose in many ways: by occasionally appealing in the claimant's interest, by often seeking further evidence favourable to the claimant on the latter's appeal, and in a suitable case by supporting his appeal. In all cases their submissions are obviously intended to set out the case fairly. They always produce all the relevant evidence no matter which way it points: I cannot remember a case where it was shown or I even had reason to suspect that the insurance officer had suppressed or intentionally withheld relevant evidence.[53]

We live in an age when some claimants and others think it permissible to express any view, however offensive or reckless, about civil servants. Insurance officers and other officers of the Department are among those who suffer from this. I have been greatly impressed by the dignity with which they endure these insults. Naturally their experience varies, and with it their skill, but all in all from what I have seen of their work—and I have seen much of it—I know that the insurance officers render excellent civil service to the cause of justice. In appeals and applications to Commissioners from decisions by a medical appeal tribunal or the Attendance Allowance Board the Secretary of State is represented by legally qualified officers from the office of the Solicitor of the Department. In my experience they maintain equally high standards. Of course sometimes they make mistakes or get into a tangle, as on occasion I did. But that leads us to another and big question: whose fault was the tangle? Is the legislation unduly complicated? Many people assert that it is but prudently refrain from suggesting how it might be improved. I propose, some may say imprudently, to suggest later some respects in which I think it defective, and to indicate ways in which I think that we might improve it.

Notes

[1] *Franks*, p. 15, para. 64.

[2] See the 1975 Act, s. 101 (5).

[3] See, *e.g.* the S.S. (D.C.Q.) regs. 1975 [S.I. 1975 No. 558], reg. 13 (5).

[4] See the S.S. (D.C.Q.) regs. 1975 [S.I. 1975 No. 558], regs. 3 and 13.

[5] Most of such rules as there are are to be found in the 1975 Act, Pt. 3, the S.S. (D.C.Q.) regs. 1975 [S.I. 1975 No. 558] and the S.S. (A.A.) regs. 1975 [S.I. 1975 No. 496]. See especially reg. 3 (1) (*a*) of the former and reg. 11 (8) of the latter.

[6] I commented on the value of these documents in a Reading which I gave in the Middle Temple Hall in November 1964 entitled " Another Experiment in Legal Procedure—National Insurance," where I described the form as an admirable piece of extra-statutory improvisation. In that Reading, copies of which can be obtained from the Middle Temple Library, I drew attention to a number of features relating to hearings by local tribunals and Commissioners.

[7] The nature of their hearing was described by Professor Harry Street in Chapter 1 of his 1968 Hamlyn Lecture entitled " Justice in the Welfare State," and many of his comments apply equally to hearings by Commissioners. Since then his description has been supplemented by the reports on the research conducted by Professor Kathleen Bell of Newcastle upon Tyne University and others into the working of certain national insurance local tribunals. (See p. 5, n. 1.) Further useful light is thrown on their work by the book *Administrative Tribunals* (1973) by

Wraith and Hutchesson, and by Professor Harry Calvert's Chap. 14 in *Justice, Discretion and Poverty* (1975–76), ed. Adler and Bradley.

[8] 1975 Act, s. 101 (5). The time can be extended by a Commissioner, but by no one else.

[9] On numerous applications for leave to appeal from a medical appeal tribunal or the Attendance Allowance Board the Commissioner has drawn attention to an arguable point in favour of the claimant which nobody else had noticed, and the appeal has eventually succeeded by virtue of it. See also p. 66.

[10] See the 1975 Act, s. 101 (5) (*b*).

[11] It has been found that if this is done earlier claimants in the heat of the moment request an oral hearing which they do not really want and will not attend, thereby wasting public money.

[12] A different insurance officer can readily take a case over from another.

[13] If necessary a second court is held in the library on the premises, and occasionally a third has been held in a Commissioner's room.

[14] The subject of Decision C.P.6/74 (not reported).

[15] In a considerable number of cases trade union representatives appearing before me have started their addresses with words such as "May it please the Commission" or "Gentlemen," showing that they did not appreciate that the tribunal consisted of one person.

[16] Not long after my appointment, when it was much less common than it is now for women to wear trousers on formal occasions, a woman claimant attended a hearing wearing trousers. In view of some comments which had been made elsewhere on this matter doubt was felt in the office whether I should object. My ruling was as follows: "The Commissioners' jurisdiction extends to Scotland as well as England, and if men can wear skirts in Scotland I see no reason why women should not wear trousers in England." So wearing trousers she presented her case, and if my recollection is correct she won.

[17] See the S.S. (D.C.Q.) regs. 1975 [S.I. 1975 No. 558], reg. 3 (3). I referred to this problem in para. 9 of Decision R(I) 13/74; the full decision is Decision C.I. 16/74.

[18] See the Legal Advice and Assistance Act 1972, Pt. I, now replaced by the Legal Aid Act 1974, ss. 1–4.

[19] *McKenzie* v. *McKenzie* [1971] P. 33.

[20] See Decision R(G) 1/73, paras. 30 and 31.

[21] See the second half of House of Commons Paper 20 entitled "Legal Aid and Advice—Report of the Law Society and Comments and Recommendations of the Lord Chancellor's Advisory Committee 1973–74 Twenty Fourth Report" dated October 24, 1974, para. 41, p. 52.

[22] See p. 134.

[23] See p. 137.

[24] 1852 in 1974.

[25] See pp. 4–5.

[26] In 1974 the 189 local tribunals heard over 28,500 cases, and in some recent years the figure has been higher.

[27] I have excluded from consideration as being premature the introduction of the mobility allowance, which will affect four of the five types of proceeding.

[28] See the Report (n. 20 above), para. 46, p. 53.

[29] The Report, p. 50.

[30] An interesting note in the L.A.G. Bulletin for Nov. 1975, pp. 284–285 suggests to me that what the C.A.B. are doing in Newcastle upon Tyne is just right.

[31] The 1975 Act, s. 115 and Sched. 13; the N.I. Acts 1946, s. 43 (5), and 1965, s. 75 (2), and the I.I. Acts 1946, s. 51 (1), and 1965, s. 50 (2).

[32] See the S.S. (D.C.Q.) regs. 1975 [S.I. 1975 No. 558], reg. 6 (3); for earlier regs. see the N.I. (D.C.Q.) regs. 1948 [S.I. 1948 No. 1144], reg. 3 (3) and the N.I. (D.C.Q.) (No. 2) regs. 1967 [S.I. 1967 No. 1570], reg. 2 (3).

[33] *Franks* (para. 92), recommended that the power should be available.

[34] See, *e.g.* Decision R(U) 2/60.

[35] Decision C.P. 4/74 (not reported), para. 38.

[36] See the article " Injustice in the Welfare State " by L. W. D. Aitcheson, one of the local tribunal chairmen, in the *Journal of the Law Society of Scotland*, February 1975, Vol. 20, No. 2, p. 52 but also Professor A. W. Bradley's further article in Vol. 20, No. 6, p. 207.

[37] See the 1975 Act, Sched. 13, para. 5, and Decision C.P. 4/74 (not reported), para. 37, where it was held that it was a matter for the discretion of the statutory authority whether to take evidence on oath or not. See also *Franks*, para. 91.

[38] It may be helpful to draw attention to the following: the Acts and regulations referred to in nn. 31 and 32, above; the N.I. (I.I.) (D.C.Q.) regs. 1948 [S.I. 1948 No. 1299], reg. 2 (3) and (No. 2) regs. 1967 [S.I. 1967 No. 1571], reg. 2 (3); the judgment of Willmer L.J. in the *Moore* case [1965] 1 Q.B. 456 at p. 474; Decision R(I) 4/65 appendix (until which it had been assumed that " inquiry " was limited to an inquiry on behalf of the Minister in relation to a minister's question); the 1975 Act, ss. 114 and 115 (especially (4)); the S.S. (D.C.Q.) regs. 1975 [S.I. 1975 No. 558], particularly regs. 3 and 6; and *Spackman* v. *G.M.C.* [1943] A.C. 627.

[39] See the N.I. (I.I.) (D.C.Q.) regs. 1948 [S.I. 1948 No. 1299], reg. 22 (6); the N.I. (D.C.Q.) regs. 1955 [S.I. 1955 No. 1788], reg. 3 and the 1975 Act, s. 101 (6).

[40] In the *Burpitt* case the Court had declined to consider medical dictionaries but on the strength of general dictionaries had held that hands were " paired organs." Some doctors think that in medical parlance hands are not organs at all.

[41] See the *Jones* case [1962] 2 Q.B. 677 at pp. 688–689.

[42] Originally under the N.I. (I.I.) (D.C.Q.) regs. 1948 [S.I. 1948 No. 1299], reg. 26 (1), now under the 1975 Act, s. 101 (7).

[43] The 1975 Act like earlier Acts contains an express power to make regulations " for extending and defining the functions of assessors " for the purposes of the Act; See the 1975 Act, s. 115 and Sched. 13, para. 9.

[44] See *Richardson* v. *Redpath Brown and Co. Limited* [1944] A.C. 62 at p. 71, 36 B.W.C.C. 259 at 266.

[45] See now the S.S. (I.I.) (P.D.) regs. 1975 [S.I. 1975 No. 1537], reg. 49 (4) and Sched. 2, para. 2 (*a*).

[46] See, *e.g.* the D.H.S.S. Annual Report for 1974, p. 101, para. 10.5 and similar statements in reports for earlier years.

[47] S.S. (I.I.) (P.D.) regs. 1975 [S.I. 1975 No. 1537], Sched. 2.

[48] See the answer on Dec. 19, 1975, in the House of Commons by Mr. O'Malley, Minister of State at the D.H.S.S. to a question by Mr. Golding (*cf.* the *Guardian*, Dec. 31, 1975).

[49] See n. 53, below.

[50] Copies of the Red and Blue Books and the reported decisions are kept in the court room for the claimant's use.

[51] In unemployment benefit cases, the Department of Employment.

[52] See the judgment of Diplock L.J. (as he then was) in the *Moore* case.

[53] This tradition differs from that which prevails in some other quarters. The Annual Statement of the General Council of the Bar 1972–73, p. 26, contained the following ruling: " Counsel is under no duty to disclose to a Medical Appeal Tribunal in a case concerning the cause of an industrial injury a medical opinion given by an eminent specialist which is contrary to his client's contention." Boulton, *Conduct and Etiquette at the Bar* (6th ed., 1975), p. 78. I think that it is a matter for serious consideration whether in proceedings in the nature of an inquiry designed to ascertain the truth, whatever it may be, the claimant whilst taking advantage of the fact that the Department and the insurance officer will produce evidence supporting the claim should be allowed to withhold evidence in his possession which does the reverse.

CHAPTER SEVEN

COMMISSIONERS' DECISIONS

A Commissioner's decision has to be in writing and signed by him. It is therefore not practicable to give it at the end of an oral hearing, though on appropriate occasions the claimant is sometimes told at the hearing what the result will be. Since April 1975 the regulations have provided that the Commissioner must give reasons.[1] This merely confirms the existing practice: I have never heard of a Commissioner's decision which did not do so. Commissioners have on occasion given a decision without reasons, stating that they would follow,[2] which later they did. This practice is convenient where a hearing shortly before a holiday calls for a long statement of reasons, which will not be ready until after the holiday. If the decision is favourable to the claimant it not merely sets his mind at rest as soon as possible but also enables the decision to be implemented more quickly. I hope that the new regulation is deliberately worded as it is to enable this useful practice to continue.

The Act says merely that an appeal lies to a Commissioner from any decision of a local tribunal.[3] It gives no indication as to the form of the decision or what order the Commissioner may make. The local tribunal's decision may have been on a question only and not on a claim. In a proper case the Commissioner limits his decision to the question only, but in recent years it has become more and more the consistent practice to require the insurance officer in most cases on a claimant's appeal to a Commissioner to put forward all the objections that there may be to the claim, so as to enable the Commissioner to dispose of the whole matter once and for all.[4] However, this may not be possible, and an interim decision is sometimes given.

In the absence of any clue in the Act as to the type of decision which the Commissioner might give, a Tribunal of

Commissioners in 1963 laid down [5] in the broadest terms that where there had been some irregularity in the procedure of the local tribunal the Commissioner has a complete discretion either to remit the case for rehearing or to decide it himself. I hope that I am not being unduly immodest when I claim that this decision has had most beneficial effects. There are some cases where the local knowledge of the local tribunal applied after they have heard the evidence is of the utmost value; in others the question is more one of law where disposal by the Commissioner is just and more convenient.

The consideration by a Commissioner of an appeal from a local tribunal being by way of a rehearing in the widest sense, though fresh evidence is not necessary, evidence not given at an earlier stage is admissible, but of course it has to be weighed carefully. The situation is therefore completely different from that under the Workmen's Compensation Acts where the Court of Appeal and the House of Lords would not interfere if there was evidence before the arbitrator and no misdirection by him.[6]

On appeals and applications from a medical appeal tribunal or the Attendance Allowance Board the situation is completely different, the right of appeal being on a question of law only. The regulations enable the Commissioner to require the tribunal or board to find further facts to enable him to determine the question of law. This power has however been used hardly ever, if at all. A medical appeal tribunal is a fluctuating body not in permanent session. Its members if reassembled might well have forgotten the case. From the start the Commissioners have taken the view that a far more effective remedy, where there has been some procedural irregularity or error of law or even merely an insufficient statement of reasons,[7] is simply to set aside the decision and remit the case for rehearing, usually stating that it should be by a body differently constituted.

As to the form of decision, I always adhered to the practice which I inherited from my predecessors of putting the result of every decision in the first paragraph. This is helpful to the many claimants who cannot take in more than a paragraph or two; and it would have been invidious for me to try to distinguish between those who could and those who could not.

One rule to which I adhered rigidly in my later years was never to use Latin or Greek words. I do not think that it helps the average claimant to be told that the arguments which he has been passionately advancing are *nihil ad rem* because *ex hypothesi cadit quaestio* in view of the *locus classicus* to which the insurance officer has referred; though it might have been different if the matter had been *res integra.* (I must not digress on a little theory of my own that some Latin legal expressions enshrine " *res indigestae.*")

A Commissioner's decision can be reviewed, not in the first instance, as some think, by a Commissioner, but by an insurance officer, from whose decision there are the usual rights of appeal to a local tribunal and a Commissioner. The grounds of review are narrower in the case of a Commissioner's decision than those of an insurance officer or local tribunal.[8] Opinions and practices have differed in the past as to whether a Commissioner has power to set aside his own or another Commissioner's decision. Where there has been some accident such as the loss of a letter in the post resulting in a mis-trial the sensible course obviously was for a Commissioner to set aside the decision without putting the claimant to the trouble and cost of High Court proceedings. This is what in practice was usually done. The situation has now been clarified by regulations.[9]

Important problems arise in connection with the use of decisions of the Commissioners as precedents. Only a minute proportion of the questions arising in this branch of the law reach the Supreme Court. The decisions of the Commissioners therefore form numerically the main body of case law governing it.[10] The Franks Committee recommended that appellate tribunals should publish " leading " decisions and circulate them to lower tribunals,[11] and the importance of this is now generally recognised. In view of the number of Commissioners' decisions (of the order of 2,000 in most years) the selection of the " leading " ones for publication presents problems. This selection process is reflected in the titles of the decisions, which fall into three categories: reported, numbered and unnumbered decisions. A little later on I will explain the meanings of these categories and the significance of the various titles.[12] The task of selecting the decisions to be reported from among the numbered decisions, or very rarely the unnumbered ones, is undertaken by the Chief Commissioner, this being one of the instances where it is accepted that he speaks for the whole body of Commissioners; after seeking such advice as he thinks fit he decides which decisions shall be reported. This involves trying to steer a middle course between on the one hand creating another wagon-load of cases for the statutory authorities to study, and on the other hand failing to provide sufficient guidance on debatable points. Sometimes part only of a decision is reported on a particular point, but as every reported decision is also numbered the whole decision is normally available, though it will have received a much more limited circulation than the reported part.[13] Of course there will always be differences of opinion as to which decisions should be reported; that is inevitable.

The purpose of reporting decisions is to secure uniformity of treatment of claimants at all levels. The Commissioners have therefore from the outset repeatedly explained that their decisions are binding on local tribunals as well as insurance officers and must be followed[14] even if inconsistent with another unreported decision which they prefer, though in such a case it would not be improper for them to suggest to the claimant that he might wish to appeal to a Commissioner. A Commissioner normally follows a decision of another Commissioner unless completely satisfied that it is incorrect.[15] It has always been maintained that the doctrine of "*stare decisis*" (which I must hastily translate as meaning "standing by what has been decided") does not apply to Commissioners' decisions.

Certain decisions, the first of which was in 1953,[16] are stated at the head to be "Medical Decisions." They contain a summary of medical evidence which the statutory authorities in deciding cases of a similar type may find it useful to consider together with any other medical evidence put before them in any particular case. These decisions have served a most useful purpose, and reference to them was approved by the Court of Appeal in the *Moore* case, where the issue was one of causation. Nevertheless care is necessary in using them in any case where there is even a possibility that the opinions expressed in them may be out of date.[17]

Some of the decisions of Commissioners were the subject of an interesting experiment designed to ascertain the value of computers in retrieving case law.[18] The results suggest the value of the human brain and the computer working together and complementing each other, but I am not aware whether any practical use has been made of these results.

Titles and Citation of Decisions

As there has been, not surprisingly, a good deal of misunderstanding as to the significance of the titles of decisions of Commissioners and the correct method of citing them I hope that the following description may be useful.[19]

I have referred to the selection process,[20] which is reflected in the titles of the decisions. Since the beginning of 1951 they have been divided into reported, numbered and unnumbered decisions. The system was different down to the end of 1950 and must be referred to briefly later.

The present procedure is as follows. When the papers relating to an appeal are received in the Commissioners' office they are put in a file and the appeal is allotted a number. This consists of two (or in Scottish or Welsh cases three) letters followed by a figure, an oblique stroke and then a figure representing the year. The first letter is always C (for Commissioner). The last letter is either U, P, S, I, F, A, M or G, according to whether the claim was for unemployment benefit, a pension, sickness or invalidity benefit, industrial injuries benefit, a family allowance, an attendance allowance, a mobility allowance, or some other benefit (G for general). If the case is a Scottish or Welsh case the letter S or W is inserted between the two other letters. Thus File C.S.I. 1/75 is the file for the first Scottish appeal in an industrial injuries case received in the office during the year 1975. The large majority of files contain decisions which are of no interest for the purpose of future cases, but they are preserved. If it should be necessary later to refer to the decision it is referred to by the above number as the decision on Commissioner's File so and so. In a small proportion of the cases however the author of the decision may select it or agree to its selection for inclusion in the numbered series as having some point which might be of interest in a future case. Thus the decision on Commissioner's File C.I. 134/64 (the well-known *Dowling* case) became Decision C.I. 46/64. If nothing further had happened it would have been cited as Decision C.I. 46/64 (not reported) instead of the decision on File C.I. 134/64. But in fact something more did happen. I decided that it should be reported. When a decision is reported it receives a completely different title consisting of the letter R (for reported) followed by U, P or S, etc. in brackets, followed by a consecutive number, a stroke and the year. Decision C.I. 46/64 became a reported decision,[21] Decision R(I) 16/66. The 16 means that the decision was the sixteenth decision in an industrial injuries case to be reported during the year 1966. The effect of the decision's being reported is that it is printed by H.M. Stationery Office, unlike other decisions which are merely duplicated. It is given a far wider circulation, which includes local tribunals and local offices of the Department. A reported decision indicates in the heading if the case comes from Scotland.[22] The headnote of a reported decision is not part of the decision and is not prepared in the Commissioners' office.

Where proceedings are taken in the High Court in connection with a decision, if the High Court judgment contains any matter which may be of importance in a future case the modern practice is to report the Commissioner's decision, if this has not already been done, with the judgments in the High Court printed as an appendix. This has been found to be very convenient to those who have ready access to the reported decisions of the Commissioners but not to the law reports.

Before 1951 the system was different. Every decision was included in what now constitute the volumes of numbered decisions. A few were picked out and reported, the letters K.L. or simply K. being added to the title. The meaning of these letters has now been forgotten, so they are not now used.

The correct method of citing Commissioners' decisions is therefore as follows:

(a) *Decisions after 1950.*

(1) *Reported.* Cited as Decision R(I) 16/66 or Commissioner's Decision R(I) 16/66, according to the context.

(2) *Numbered.* Cited as Decision C.I. 1/75 (not reported).

(3) *Unnumbered.* Cited as the decision on Commissioner's File C.A. 1/75.

(b) *Decisions before 1951.*

(1) *Reported or K. or K.L.* Cited as Decision C.U. 3/48 (reported).

(2) *Unreported.* Cited as Decision C.U. 4/48 (not reported).

In all the citations beginning with the letter C (but not those beginning with R) there will be an S or a W added after it if the decision is in a Scottish or Welsh case.

Many years ago it was represented to me that the insurance officers had an unfair advantage in having access to the numbered decisions and also knowing who was the author of each decision. As a result it was arranged that a complete set of the numbered decisions (from 1948) other than the reported ones should be available in each of the Commissioners' three offices for inspection by anybody interested, and that on request copies should be supplied within reasonable limits. Further, for many years the name of the author of a decision, whether reported or not, has appeared at the end of it. I at the same time directed that if anyone inquired who was the author of any Commissioner's decision (back to 1948) which did not show it he should be told.

Quite apart from these arrangements the practice is that if the insurance officer in any appeal refers to a decision other than a reported one he supplies the claimant with a copy of it.

Notes

[1] See the S.S. (D.C.Q.) regs. 1975 [S.I. 1975 No. 558], reg. 13 (6). None of the earlier regulations contained a requirement to give reasons.

[2] *e.g.* Decision R(I) 8/68.

[3] See the 1975 Act, s. 101.

[4] A disqualification under s. 19 or s. 20 of the 1975 Act may cover a period for which a claim has not yet been made. As to forward allowances and disallowances see the S.S. (Claims and Payments) regs. 1975 [S.I. 1975 No. 560], regs. 11 and 12. See also Decision C.S. 2/76.

[5] Decision R(U) 3/63, which contains a number of examples of irregularities which despite everyone's efforts had occurred in different cases.

[6] Numerous Commissioners' decisions on their jurisdiction and procedure are helpfully collected in J 192 to 202.

[7] As to reasons see the S.S. (D.C.Q.) regs. 1975 [S.I. 1975 No. 558], regs. 12 and 23 and the S.S. (A.A.) regs. 1975 [S.I. 1975 No. 496], reg. 9 (2).

[8] See the 1975 Act, s. 104 (1) (*a*).

[9] See the S.S. (Correction and Setting Aside of Decisions) regs. 1975 [S.I. 1975 No. 572]. These regulations also usefully incorporate a slip rule. I do not claim that it was anything but a coincidence that this rule did not come into force until the first working day after I retired.

[10] See p. 124, below.

[11] See *Franks*, para. 102.

[12] A curious effect of the changes of name in 1966 (see p. 13, above) is that there are printed volumes of reported Commissioner's Decisions until 1968 and Commissioners' Decisions thereafter.

[13] See pp. 75–77, above.

[14] See numerous cases collected in J 1055 to 1056 under "Precedents."

[15] See, *e.g.* Decisions R(G) 3/62, paras. 13 and 14, and R(U) 3/67.

[16] Decision R(I) 37/53.

[17] See Decision R(I) 12/68 and pp. 130–131, below.

[18] See Colin Tapper, *Computers and the Law* (1973), Weidenfeld and Nicolson, London.

[19] *Cf.* the note in the L.A.G. Bulletin for Dec. 1974 at p. 300, which is substantially correct.

[20] See pp. 73–74, above.

[21] The Jenkins Index contains reported but not numbered decisions. Much useful information on reported decisions is to be found in its Introduction and Appendix I, and in the introductory notes to the various bound volumes of Commissioner's decisions.

[22] This is done as a matter of routine in case the decision touches on an area of law where the law of Scotland differs from that of England. This reason does not apply in a Welsh case.

CHAPTER EIGHT

COMPLEXITY OF THE LEGISLATION

FROM time to time it is alleged that the legislation administered by the Commissioners is too bulky, inconveniently arranged and complicated. The critics, even if they do not betray a marked ignorance of the contents of it, hardly ever make any constructive suggestions as to its improvement. Nevertheless I think that there is sufficient truth in some of the charges to justify considering them.

I do not myself think that there is much in the charge of bulkiness in itself. Parliament has laid down what benefits shall be available. The law has to govern the payment of thousands of millions of pounds annually [1] to millions of people whose circumstances vary enormously. There must necessarily be many different rules designed to cover different cases. They must inevitably occupy a considerable amount of space in the legislation. Some streamlining may be possible, but I doubt whether it would result in much reduction in bulk. Indeed one of the criticisms of the legislation has been of excessive compression.

In discussing complexity one must remember in fairness to all concerned with the preparation of legislation that the 1965 and 1975 Acts were merely consolidations, which of course very strictly limited the changes that could be made, though in fact each had been preceded by legislation specifically designed to pave the way for consolidation.[2]

In considering these allegations I am not concerned to discuss whether particular benefits ought to exist or not; those are matters for politicians. What I am considering is whether the rules governing the receipt of the different benefits give effect as clearly, simply and conveniently as possible to the intentions of Parliament. These questions are very important, since complexity in itself can lead to injustice.

How complicated is it reasonable for a statute to be? The answer may depend on whose interests are being considered mainly. The interests of the makers are different from those of the person who, not being a maker, has to use the legislation, to whom for brevity I will refer as "the user." Some few of these are lawyers: members of the legal profession (including members of the legal departments of trade unions), chairmen of tribunals, Commissioners and the judges. The large majority are laymen: many trade union and other representatives, two of the three members of each tribunal, the Attendance Allowance Board and their delegates, and above all the insurance officers, who decide 10,000 cases for every one decided by a Commissioner and a few million for every one decided by a court. The maker and the user both want provisions which are clear and certain, but they differ in that some of the makers are familiar with the whole of the particular portion of the law and know where to find each provision, whereas the user may be seriously inconvenienced if he has to search in different parts of statutes and regulations. An important question therefore is whose interests should a statute consider. My own view is emphatic. I think that the words which all of those concerned in the preparation of legislation should have in the forefront of their minds are: "Think always of the user."

On this question of simplification we are fortunate in having available the completely up-to-date report of the committee set up under the chairmanship of Sir David Renton Q.C., M.P., to consider the question.[3] For brevity I will refer to it simply as *Renton.* Many of their recommendations are directly relevant to the subject matter of my lectures and it is to be hoped that effect will be given to them. I was particularly pleased to read their recommendations that in principle the interests of the ultimate users should always have priority over those of the legislators; a Bill should be regarded primarily as a future Act; and the needs of the eventual user must be given priority over those of the legislator when proposals for amending existing legislation are being framed.[4]

During 16 years' work as a Commissioner I noticed numerous instances where the recommendations now made by the Renton Committee appeared to be disregarded in a variety of ways. Sometimes the ideas expressed by the words were excessively complicated. Sometimes simple ideas were expressed in complex language. Sometimes the arrangement and order were such as to involve the user in a wholly disproportionate amount of work discovering provisions scattered over different parts of the legislation. These were matters of form. There were also matters of substance, where it seemed doubtful whether the way in which the legislation was expressed was resulting in giving effect to what Parliament apparently intended. Since these matters of form and substance to some extent overlap I will give some examples, but I must first say this. If one collects together a number of things which one thinks are wrong or on further investigation may be found to be wrong, one may give the impression of thinking that everything is wrong. That is certainly not my view. Many of the provisions work perfectly well, and nobody outside those directly concerned ever hears about them. The provisions which are the troublemakers crop up again and again.

I think that some of the most important and difficult problems arise under the sections dealing with industrial injuries benefits.[5] Their main broad purpose is to compensate everyone covered by the scheme who is injured as a result of his employment. The Workmen's Compensation Act test of liability, whether the workman had suffered " personal injury by accident arising out of and in the course of his employment " had given rise to what has been described as the wagon-load of cases, but it was incorporated in the Industrial Injuries Act 1946.[6] This adoption has not been entirely successful. In an age when the meaning of the word " employment " is continually expanding, opinions are likely to differ as to what in fact is " incidental to " it.[7]

The exact effects of the presence of the words " by accident " and in particular the question whether the phrase " personal injury by accident " is equivalent to " accidental injury " or whether it means " injury by *an* accident " have been much discussed. Under the 1975 Act, as under its predecessors, the periods of title to injury benefit and disablement benefit are described by reference to " *the* relevant accident," and indeed that phrase is defined in the statutes.[8] Against this background it is not surprising that the doctrine of Process survives and defeats a substantial number of claims, which in my opinion are deserving claims. I regard the doctrine as a most unfortunate consequence of the wording of the Act. If a man can prove a single accident he wins. If he proves a number of accidents he may win by virtue of the doctrine accepted by the House of Lords in *Selvage* v. *Burrell*.[9] If however the events which cause his disability were countless and spread over a long period he will probably lose as a result of the doctrine of Process. If those events constitute a prescribed disease he may win with the help (usually) of a presumption,[10] provided that he is in the right occupation. But there are many people in the wrong occupation, and as the history of the events leading up to the prescription of deafness for certain occupations shows, prescription may be a slow process and incomplete. In a recent case [11] the claimant was deafened by noise made not by him but by others, close to whom he had to work. It was held by the majority of a Tribunal of Commissioners that deafness was not prescribed in relation to him. So his claim failed. If the decision of the majority is not challenged and represents what the law is, I am most positively of opinion that it is not what it ought to be. My view is that a claimant should be entitled to rely on three grounds: first, injury by accident if he can prove it; secondly, prescribed disease, as at present, with the help (usually) of the statutory presumption; and thirdly, injury caused by his employment if he can prove that.[12]

" Arising out of " raises a question of causation. " In the course of " raises a question mainly of time and place though with overtones of purpose and causation. Over the first dozen years of the Commissioners' administration of industrial injuries law various hard or controversial cases arose; indeed some such cases had already emerged during the workmen's compensation period. " Arising out of " now causes comparatively little difficulty, because Parliament in 1961 successfully identified most of the hard cases under this head and simply enacted that in those cases the accident should be deemed to arise out of the employment.[13] I think that this was one of the most satisfactory pieces of legislation ever enacted in this field. It is based on an idea which is so good that it could be used elsewhere. It is to enact something in general terms, *e.g.* that entitlement shall depend on showing that the accident arose out of and in the course of the employment, but to couple this with a deeming provision relating to certain particular instances where everyone feels that there ought to be entitlement but the circumstances do not fit happily into the general phrase: though not to deem something which everyone knows to be absurd.

Unfortunately Parliament has never succeeded in giving the same treatment to " in the course of." I am not aware that it has ever tried, or that the Industrial Injuries Advisory Council has ever been invited to conduct a wide-ranging inquiry into the boundaries of the course of the employment. Whether such questions have been considered within the Department and with what result I do not know. The fact is that a steady flow of disputed " in the course of " cases comes before the Commissioners, many of them indicating strong dissatisfaction on the part of sensible and reputable claimants, which is evidence that the statutory boundary needs looking at again. The cases are of many different kinds but some of the more important ones may be classified broadly under the following headings.

Travel causes difficulties. The general rule is clearly established that the claimant is not in the course of his employment whilst travelling on a highway to or from a fixed place of work such as a factory. (Whether this rule is satisfactory may be a different matter; in some countries it is different.) If however an employee is sent by his employers to do work at a distance and drives his own or their car with petrol supplied by his employers, and stays the night at a hotel, whose bill the employers will pay, is he in the course of his employment if he injures himself at any one of the numerous moments during his expedition which they treat as working time?

A person travelling as a passenger in a vehicle provided by his employer is deemed to be in the course of his employment but if he is himself driving the vehicle he is not. This has always seemed to me an anomaly.[13a]

In access cases, public highways are the main bogey, *e.g.*

where the employee has to cross a road, the soil of which may be vested in the employers, to get to the works or the canteen, or a coal miner to get to the pit-head baths.[13a]

Numerous recreation cases come before the Commissioners, *e.g.* of firemen awaiting a call and filling in time kicking a football around; police officers playing games as representatives of their forces; civil servants hanging up decorations for the annual office party, and so on. These examples are nothing like exhaustive; the variety of problems is enormous. The course of the employment " covers and includes things belonging to or arising out of it " [14]; or things " reasonably incidental " to it.[15] But opinions can and do differ widely as to what is " incidental." Some people would say that the journey to work ought to be so regarded. Also many people would, I think, say that, as the word employment comes to embrace more and more in addition to the actual work, so " in the course of the employment (including what is incidental to it) " should be more and more widely construed.

The decision in the recent *Michael* case [16] demonstrates how unsatisfactory the law on this topic is. It shows that the question whether an activity is reasonably incidental to a claimant's employment is a question of fact, and provided that the adjudicating authority does not misdirect itself in point of law its decision either way will not be interfered with. Some people think that this situation is inevitable and acceptable. I do not. It means that different decisions can be given in identical cases.[17] This in my opinion is unjust, and every possible step should be taken to prevent it. This cannot be done judicially. Even if a right of appeal on fact were created there would still be the possibility that the appellate judges themselves would reach different decisions on questions of fact. It would seem that the possibility of a " deeming " solution similar to that so successfully applied to " arising out of " should at least be considered.

The definition of the injury benefit period by reference to the non-availability of disablement benefit has always, especially since an amendment in 1953, seemed to me putting the cart before the horse and making the situation difficult to understand.[18] The presence of the phrase " finally determined " has added to the difficulty, as the decisions of the Commissioners both in Great Britain and Northern Ireland have demonstrated.[19]

Other provisions governing benefit for industrial injuries which in my opinion need to be looked at carefully include those which govern the decision by the medical authorities of the questions whether the accident has resulted in a loss of faculty and what the relevant loss of faculty consists of and in assessing the degree of disablement.[20] The Act and the regulations[21] lay down in considerable detail the rules for assessing the degree of disablement. The difficulties of these were highlighted in the *Cable* case, but the amendments of the regulations after that case only partly solve the difficulties. The Act directs a comparison between the claimant's physical and mental condition and that of " a person of the same age and sex whose physical and mental condition is normal."[22] Where the injury is a crude physical one such as a fracture this may be workable, but in other cases with what sort of normal person does the medical board make the comparison? With a farmer, an office worker or whom? If a person of outstanding intellect or physique suffers an injury which reduces his intelligence or physique to that of a normal person, is he not disabled at all? Should not the comparison be between the claimant's condition as it is and as it would have been but for the accident? The view held by some people is that this provision has survived because nobody has ever taken the slightest notice of it. In any event are not the rules excessively elaborate? Many judges and doctors are perfectly familiar with the process of forming an opinion on questions such as the extent to which a person is disabled and the extent to which his disability is attributable to an accident as opposed to extraneous circumstances.

A comparison of the forms provided by the Department with the rules contained in the statutes and regulations suggests that they speak different languages.[23] The forms ask a number of questions not in the legislation and do not ask all those to which an answer is needed: in particular they do not ask the all-important question what the relevant loss of faculty consists of.[24] If the law were reframed might it be better to adjust it to what the doctors find to be workable, rather than to preserve provisions which obviously they have found difficult to administer?

In the industrial injuries field the section which has given rise to most difficulty is section 60, well known since 1948 to all those concerned with it simply as section 14. Almost every sentence in the section has been the subject of numerous Commissioners' decisions, some of them conflicting. In a number of respects the section produces results which in my opinion are unjust. An adequate discussion of the problems must inevitably be long and somewhat technical, and in these circumstances I have devoted to it a part of the next chapter.

In the field of national insurance as opposed to industrial injuries I will refer briefly to only a few subjects.

Unemployment benefit was first introduced in 1911.[25] The present form of the provisions governing it gives the impression of a building which has been patched here and repaired there and is now the most extraordinary jumble. One would expect to find the main conditions for the receipt of the benefit in the body of the Act, minor matters and perhaps figures in the schedules, and even more minor or exceptional matters in regulations. In fact some of the most important conditions are in regulations. Thus if an unemployed person refuses a reasonable offer of employment he may be disqualified under the Act for a limited period not exceeding six weeks.[26] If however in the course of refusing he places unreasonable restrictions on the employment which he is prepared to accept, he may be disentitled under the regulations for an unlimited period.[27] Of two equally important rules, each of which can result in disentitlement, known as the " normal idle day " rule and the " full extent normal " rule one is contained in the Act and the other in regulations.[28] The justification for these distinctions is less apparent when one notes that in the case of unemployment, sickness and invalidity benefit disqualification has for benefit purposes the same effects as disentitlement,[29] though this does not apply to other benefits.[29a]

Sometimes the rules mean what they do not say or say what they do not mean. One rule provides that a day shall not be treated as a day of unemployment if on that day the person is engaged in any employment unless each of four conditions is satisfied.[30] What the regulation means however is that the day is to be treated as a day of unemployment even though the claimant is engaged in employment if he satisfies each of the four conditions.[31]

I think that it is only necessary to read through all the sections and regulations governing unemployment benefit,[32] particularly where the later part of the regulations qualifies not only the earlier part of the regulations but also the Act itself, to see the complexity of the situation. These are matters of form, but I think that the opportunity should be taken of reviewing all the rules to see whether they are still appropriate in the conditions of today. On many occasions indignation has been expressed to me by claimants who have contributed regularly for 20 or 30 years but the first time that they claim unemployment benefit they find themselves disqualified. A number of them have suggested to me that there might be something in the nature of a no claim bonus. Might this be worth considering?

Another topic where I think that the form of the statute could be greatly improved concerns retirement pensions. The present form makes it necessary for a user advising someone of a particular class, for example a spinster, to read a large amount of matter relating to other classes, to make sure that there is nothing affecting her. This again is a technical matter, and I defer discussion of it to the next chapter.

Any proposals for machinery designed to help with the improvement of the statute law must take account of the fact that there are some problems which apply to more than one of the three schemes administered by the Commissioners,[33] and indeed sometimes also to schemes outside their jurisdiction. An example of the former concerns increases of benefit, for example in respect of adult dependants. Although national insurance benefits and industrial injuries benefits are now in the same statute the provisions relating to increases of them remain separate.[34] One would have thought that more co-ordination and abbreviation could be achieved here. An example of the second type is the highly controversial cohabitation rule, which applies in relation not only to widow's benefits[35] but also to supplementary benefit, which is not administered by the Commissioners.

Particularly difficult problems have arisen in the past in relation to all of the three schemes in relation to what I may perhaps describe as the support problem. Whether the problem will be made better or worse when the Child Benefit Act 1975 comes fully into force remains to be seen. What has happened in the past has been like this. For family allowance purposes a child not living with a parent cannot be included in that parent's family unless the cost of providing for the child is contributed to by the parent at not less than a certain rate; and contributions in kind have to be taken into account. The provisions in the Act are supplemented by regulations.[36] These have in practice been found to create great difficulties. If a father ordered to contribute to the maintenance of his children paid regularly by a banker's order there would be no difficulty. What often happens is that for the first few months he pays; then his payments become irregular; then there is a huge gap; and then he sends along a nice winter overcoat for one of the children. In such a case to what extent was the cost of providing for how many children at what rate over what period contributed to by the father? Worse however was to come. The national insurance scheme and the industrial injuries scheme each provided for increases of benefit in respect of children, but two of the conditions were that the child was included in the claimant's family and that the cost of providing for the child was contributed to to a certain extent (not the same as the family allowance test extent). Each scheme had, as it still has, its own rules completely different from the family allowance rules, governing these questions of contribution. The result of this was that to decide whether an increase of benefit was payable under the national insurance or industrial injury schemes the statutory authorities had to decide both whether the case was covered by the family allowance rules so that the child could be included in the claimant's family and also whether it was covered by the other rules so that the contributions were sufficient for those purposes. There seems to be a strong case here for co-ordination.

Another problem which arises in more areas than one may be described as the " all or nothing " problem. Some increases of benefit, such as that in respect of adult dependants, are cut off abruptly if earnings exceed the prescribed amount to even a small extent.[37] Some benefits are payable in full even though the statutory ground forms only a small part of the cause of the event giving rise to the benefit, *e.g.*, industrial death benefits.[38] On the other hand there is sometimes tapering off, *e.g.*, where a retirement pensioner within five years of pensionable age has earnings above a certain amount.[39] The increase cases give rise to great dissatisfaction,[40] but the public cannot know whether it is ever considered in the Department whether these inequalities might be ironed out and why they are not.

These are only some examples of subjects which need consideration right across the board—openly.

The *Renton* Report quoted several criticisms of the drafting of statutes which they accepted as being valid. As in quoting me they transposed the verb in the sentence that I wrote, perhaps I may be permitted to record that what in fact I did write was: " . . . a statute should be not only clear and unambiguous but *readable.* It ought not to call for the exercise of a cross-word/acrostic mentality which is able to ferret out the meaning from a number of sections, schedules and regulations." [41] Lord Simon of Glaisdale referred the committee to a remarkable example from the National Insurance Acts of obscurity by maximum compression.[42] It is no longer part of the law, so I will refer to another example, which I suggest shows a progressive lack of consideration of the interests of the user. I refer to the changes over the years in the method of fixing the dates of commencement of statutes.

The user needs to know whether a statutory provision has yet come into force, and often also when it did so, particularly in the field of national insurance, where the law is changed frequently and a claim covering a period may depend on both what the law is and what it was. From the point of view of the user much the simplest method is for the Act to say nothing, so that it comes into force automatically on receiving the Royal Assent; or to state one date on which the whole of it will take effect. Barely less convenient is the method of making the appointed day a single date appointed by a very short order.[43] In this field however it has increasingly become the much less satisfactory practice for quite short statutes to have two or three or even more orders fixing numerous different dates of commencement for different purposes, even where the purpose of the statute is substantially only to increase the rates of benefit and contributions. The 1973 Act had four orders appointing dates of commencement and one further one cancelling some of the appointed dates.[44] The 1975 Act does something much more dreadful. To discover whether any provision of the 1975 Act has come into force and if so when, one needs to look first at a subsection of the Act itself, the whole of which is qualified by a subsection of the Consequential Provisions Act: the latter makes it necessary to look at a section of a 1973 Act, a paragraph in a Schedule to a 1974 Act, a section of another 1974 Act, and a paragraph of a Schedule to yet another 1975 Act; and then to discover whether any regulation has been made under a certain Schedule to the 1973 Act and also the extent to which any provision contained in the 1975 consolidations was on a certain date not yet in force and dependent for its entry into force on an order made under any of those provisions. When one looks at those provisions some of them refer to still further provisions. One's task is not made any easier by the fact that the subsection which causes all the trouble contains two phrases which might puzzle the user, one of which is defined in a section other than the interpretation section without a signpost, and the other is not defined at all except indirectly by virtue of the phrase that expressions defined in another Act have the same meaning in this Act.[45]

Probably the user will discover at the end of all this research that the qualifications on which the dates of commencement depend have nothing to do with his case. But the user cannot know that until he has found his way through this little statutory jungle. Also it is more difficult to check the non-existence of regulations than their existence, particularly when there is difficulty in obtaining them quickly from the Stationery Office.

The reason for all this seems to have been simply as follows. Before April 6, 1975, when the 1975 Act came into force, earlier Acts had provided for some new benefits but no date of commencement for the sections containing those benefits had yet been fixed. Two examples are non-contributory invalidity pension and invalid care allowance provided for by a statute enacted only a week before the 1975 Act itself.[46] (As usual, legislation in a hurry.) The 1975 Act itself contains in sections 36 and 37 provision for these benefits, though they did not come into force immediately. I cannot see why the matter could not have been dealt with perfectly simply by enacting that the 1975 Act, except sections 36, 37 and any others that there were, was to come into force on April 6, 1975, making any special provision for those sections that was appropriate. The user would then not have been put to any more trouble than glancing at sections 36, 37, etc. to make sure that they had nothing to do with him, instead of having to look at a number of statutes and check that certain regulations did not exist. Doing it this way, if in fact it was possible, would certainly have saved the user a lot of trouble.

The Social Security Conference

I pass now to the question whether any machinery should be set up to improve the preparation of social security law. I am strongly of opinion that there should be set up a standing advisory body, which when I first proposed it in 1969 I christened the Social Security Conference of Great Britain.[48] It would operate very much as the Law Commissions do, studying problems in depth, compiling working papers, publishing them, considering views expressed in reply, and after considerable discussion producing a Bill as clear and short as circumstances permit. I think that this is consistent with the views expressed by Lord Justice Scarman in his 1974 Hamlyn

Lectures, Part VII. I do not think that he could have contemplated a single body to deal with the whole of administrative law. One needs only to look at the Schedule to the Tribunals and Inquiries Act 1971 to see that the ground covered by them is enormous; and the problems of substantive law dealt with in them have in many instances nothing in common. It may be objected that the ground is covered by the bodies that we already have: the Law Commissions, the Council on Tribunals, NIAC, IIAC, the Attendance Allowance Board and the Supplementary Benefits Commission. Nobody has a greater admiration than myself for the work achieved by these bodies, but I believe the objection to be ill-founded. The Law Commissions have many other fish to fry and have not played any appreciable part in directly influencing the development of national insurance or so far as I know social security law.[49] The Council on Tribunals are concerned with procedure only, but in my opinion it is the substantive law which needs looking at. The scope of NIAC and IIAC is strictly limited: they can only advise on the amending of statutes if invited to do so, and as I shall show the part that NIAC have been allowed to play in relation to regulations has been gradually eroded over the years.[50] Further, and this is of capital importance, there never has been a family allowances advisory committee, and child benefit under the Child Benefit Act 1975 will not be a benefit under the 1975 Act, so NIAC will not be able to operate in relation to it. Also national insurance does not come within the terms of reference of any other law reform body. When in 1970 attendance allowances were introduced the duty of advising the Secretary of State on the working of the 1970 Act in respect of them, as well as deciding individual claims, was entrusted to the Attendance Allowance Board.[51] Thus a further separate advisory body was created.

The result is that there is no one body outside the Department empowered to advise over the whole field, with a view to making the systems work harmoniously as a consistent whole without either gaps or overlapping, and to eliminate the results of hurried legislation,[52] which is chronic in the national insurance field. The creation of such a body would have numerous advantages. It would go far to bring out more into the open the discussions preceding legislation, which at present are behind closed doors. It would be essential that it should have a free hand to consider all problems of social security law and procedure, though as it would be merely an advisory body the government of the day could reject any of its proposals. It would need to be strong in lawyers[53] and others having practical experience of the actual administration of the relevant branches of the law and also some neighbouring ones, since taxation and the rules relating to overlapping benefits affect the amount of money which the beneficiary actually gets.[54] If anyone is interested in my views in detail they are available to him. During the winter of 1969–70 I approached the Secre-

MICKLETHWAIT HAMLYN LECTURE

Errata

On page 92, line 30, should read: " respect of them, as well as deciding individual questions, was ".

the National Insurance Advisory Committee, as is shown by the history of the legislation affecting that committee.

This has happened in several ways. The 1946 Act required that the Minister should submit a draft of any regulations (with specified exceptions immaterial to this discussion) to NIAC and that they should give public notice of the draft and consider any comments on it before advising the Minister.[57] A practice grew up of including in any amending Act a provision excluding these requirements when the draft was laid before Parliament within six months of the passing of the amending Act, if the regulations stated that they were made *in consequence of* that Act. Such a provision has now been made a permanent part of the law unless expressly excluded.[58] Advantage was taken of this exclusion to make a regulation which was not put before NIAC, and of which consequently public notice did not have to be given. Though the regulation was less favourable to claimants than the amending Act enabled it to be, the justification for the difference was claimed to be found in the 1946 Act.[59] This seems to me a most unsatisfactory state of affairs.

In 1973 the requirement of public notice inconspicuously disappeared and has never been reinstated.[60] I believe that in practice NIAC do give public notice, but a legal right is something different from a discretionary power.

Finally, there has been introduced into the rules governing NIAC a provision, always present in those governing the Industrial Injuries Advisory Council,[61] that regulations need not be submitted to NIAC if by reason of the urgency of the matter the Secretary of State thinks it inexpedient.[62] In view of the haste in which modern legislation is conceived and enacted it seems probable that this exception will be much relied on, as indeed it was to a massive extent in the making in 1975 of the regulations associated with the consolidations of that year.[63] There is a separate exclusion for regulations which merely consolidate.[64]

The Form of Legislation

As to the form of the legislation, there should in my opinion be one basic Act for a subject of suitable size such as national insurance, industrial injuries and family allowances or child benefit.[65] This would involve a complete consolidation. The basic Act would be designed to be as permanent as anything in this world can be. It would provide a framework to contain the provisions for the existing and future benefits and contributions. Each of the benefits would retain its section number(s) permanently. New benefits would be slotted in by way of textual amendment.[66] If to preserve the section numbers of the others these had to have section numbers ending with letters, fractions or decimals, we should not be worried about doing that. If a benefit were abolished that would leave a gap, but that would not matter.[67] Acts should be available also in loose-leaf form. The Red Book and the Blue Book have pointed the direction in which we should go. The reprinting not only of the whole basic Act but also of the changed portions of it, as has been done with those books, would provide a less expensive way of enabling the user to keep his copy up to date. An amending Act would contain nothing of any importance that was not slotted into the basic Act. If temporary provisions were necessary to cover transitional or other matters some device would have to be invented such as inserting into the basic Act a new schedule, which could be repealed as a whole when it was spent. An essential result would be that the user could safely assume that the up-to-date reprint of the Act represented the whole of the statute law and he need not look either backwards or forwards in case there were more. These are merely particular instances in support of my proposition that the makers of legislation need to give a far higher priority than they do to the user's convenience. The laws are the marching orders of all of us citizens, and they should be made as easy as possible for us to understand.

What has in fact happened is as follows. Between the enactment of the original statutes in 1945 and 1946 and the first consolidation in 1965 some 20 further statutes were passed. Some of them inserted sections by way of textual amendment; others dealt with the situation by other means. This made it impossible for a user to be certain that the basic Act had not been modified by some later statute, a difficulty which was acute before the first publication of the Red and Blue Books in 1961 and still existed to some extent after it. The 1965 consolidations altered the numbers of most of the sections. Between 1965 and the next consolidations in 1975 there were over 20 further statutes, some of which again proceeded by way of textual amendment, though others did not, with similar consequences all over again.

The 1975 Act contains an admirable innovation, the inventor of which should be warmly congratulated. For the interpretation of expressions in the Act one has to look, not for a section placed in the usual inconspicuous position near the end of the sections and before the schedules, but at a glossary in the last Schedule, which is as easy to find as the index of a book. It seems to me that general use should be made of this excellent idea.

I have already indicated my view that consolidation should be created complete and kept complete. Unfortunately this has not happened with the 1975 consolidations. Portions of the 1973 Act are left in force despite them.[68] Some of those portions together with parts of the 1975 Act have since been repealed, and some others amended, sometimes by way of textual amendment and sometimes not, by the Social Security Pensions Act 1975. But here again care is necessary, since there are four commencement orders bringing parts of this last Act into force on various dates ranging between August 1975 and April 1979.[69] In fact within a few months of the incomplete 1975 consolidations they had become appreciably further unconsolidated, but to discover the extent to which this has happened one has to search. To find out the statute law of national insurance one has to examine four Acts, the 1973 Act, the 1975 Act, the Consequential Provisions Act and the Social Security Pensions Act 1975, and the various statutory instruments under them including those by which they have been or will be brought into force from time to time. In this search some legal publications are a very great help,[70] but national insurance is pre-eminently a branch of the law where it is wholly wrong that the user should be put to the expense of buying law books, few of which are cheap today, or going to the trouble of obtaining access to them by other means.

Child benefit introduced since the 1975 consolidations by the Child Benefit Act 1975 will be a separate benefit and not one under the Social Security Act 1975; the opportunity has not been taken of merging this benefit, which replaces family allowances, into the Social Security Act scheme. This Act when brought into force will also contain some provisions affecting the 1975 Act otherwise than by way of textual amendment.

My conclusions in broad terms on the whole matter are these. In accordance with the *Renton* recommendations the needs of the user should be given priority both in original legislation and amendments. There should be a basic Act (or Acts) containing the statute law in its most convenient form and order. It should form the permanent framework of national insurance law. Once it has been enacted, changes should be effected only by textual amendment, and in such a way as not to alter the numbers of the existing sections, schedules, etc. Much the best chance of achieving this would result from setting up an advisory body covering the whole field of social security. Such a body might be able more publicly to provide the basis of something nearer to a multi-partisan policy, and we might be able to escape not only some of the worst consequences of legislation in a hurry but also the waste of money which occurs whenever a new government scraps wholly or in part a Bill produced at great expense by its predecessors, such as Mr. Crossman's 1969 Bill and parts of the 1973 Act.

Notes

[1] See pp. 4–5, above.

[2] The National Insurance &c. Act 1964 and the Social Security Amendment Act 1974.

[3] " The Preparation of Legislation," Cmnd. 6053.

[4] See *Renton,* recommendations 8, 14, 19 and 39.

[5] The 1975 Act, Pt. II, Chaps. IV and V.

[6] See the I.I. Acts 1946, ss. 1 and 7, and 1965, ss. 1 and 5; now the 1975 Act, s. 50.

[7] See the *Culverwell* case, n. 15, below.

[8] See the 1975 Act, s. 57 and Sched. 20.

[9] (1921) 14 B.W.C.C. 158.

[10] See the S.S. (I.I.) (P.D.) regs. 1975 [S.I. 1975 No. 1537], reg. 4 and Sched. 1, Pt. 1, para. 48.

[11] See Decision R(I) 15/75.

[12] See Decision R(I) 7/66, para. 15.

[13] See the F.A.N.I. Act 1961, s. 2; now the 1975 Act, s. 55.

[13a] See J 1538–1580.

[14] See *St. Helens Colliery Co. Ltd.* v. *Hewitson* [1924] A.C. 59 at p. 71.

[15] See the *Culverwell case* [1966] 2 Q.B. 21 at pp. 48F and 49E.

[16] See *The Times,* Dec. 20, 1975; (1976) 126 N.L.J. 114.

[17] See Decisions C.I. 1/72, C.I. 7/73, and C.I. 7/74 (all unreported).

[18] See the I.I. Act 1946, ss. 11 and 12 as amended by the I.I. Act 1953, s. 3; now the 1975 Act, s. 57 (4).

[19] See *e.g.* Decisions R(I) 14/63 and R(I) 15/63.

[20] See the 1975 Act, s. 108 (1) and Sched. 8 and the *Ward* case.

[21] See the 1975 Act, Sched. 8 and the S.S. (I.I.) (Benefit) regs. 1975 [S.I. 1975 No. 559], reg. 2.

[22] See Sched. 8, para. 1 (*a*).

[23] See especially the forms in the B.I. 118 series.

[24] See the *Ward* case and pp. 104–105, below.

[25] See the N.I. Act 1911, Pt. II.

[26] See the 1975 Act, s. 20.

[27] See the S.S. (U.S.I. Benefit) regs. 1975 [S.I. 1975 No. 564], reg. 7 (1) (*a*).

[28] See the 1975 Act, s. 17 (1) (*b*) and [S.I. 1975 No. 564] (above), reg. 7 (1) (*e*) and (2).

[29] See [S.I. 1975 No. 564] (above), reg. 7 (1) (*c*) and (*d*).

[29a] We have seen (pp. 31–32, above) that a person can be entitled and not disqualified, but the benefit is not payable.

[30] See the S.S. (U.S.I. Benefit) regs. 1975 [S.I. 1975 No. 564], reg. 7 (1) (*h*).

[31] See Decision R(U) 16/64.

[32] Including those referred to on pp. 32–33, above.

[33] *e.g.* the twin obstacles of disentitlement and disqualification operate under two schemes.

[34] See the 1975 Act, Chaps. III and IV of Pt. II.

[35] See the 1975 Act, ss. 24, 25, 26 and 67.

[36] See the F.A. (Qualifications) regs. 1969 [S.I. 1969 No. 212], Pt. IV.

[37] See *e.g.* the 1975 Act, s. 44 (1) (*b*).

[38] See *e.g.* p. 115, below.

[39] See the 1975 Act, s. 30.

[40] In a different sphere the " all or nothing " rule for contributory negligence caused dissatisfaction and injustice until it was abolished by the Law Reform (Contributory Negligence) Act 1945.

[41] See *Renton*, para. 6.3, p. 28. The Report records that the whole of the evidence has been deposited in the Public Record Offices and the National Library of Wales, and I am assured that anyone can refer to it there; see *Renton*, para. 1.8, p. 3.

[42] See *Renton*, para. 6.3, p. 28, and the N.I. Act 1965, Sched. 1, Pt. II, concluding words.

[43] Used for both the big 1946 statutes.

[44] See p. 30, nn. 35 and 36, above.

[45] See the 1975 Act, s. 169 (3), *the whole* of which is qualified by the Consequential Provisions Act, s. 3 (5), which requires one to refer to numerous other statutory instruments and to discover whether or not certain regulations have been made.

[46] See the S.S. Benefits Act 1975, ss. 6 and 7.

[48] It would be for consideration whether it should be extended to cover the whole of the United Kingdom.

[49] I assume that, there being government departments immediately interested in those branches of the law, the Law Commissions have left

it to them to keep it in repair. The Law Commissions have affected matters indirectly; see *e.g.* the Nullity of Marriage Act 1971 and Decisions R(G) 1/73 and R(G) 2/73.

[50] See pp. 93–94, above.

[51] See the 1970 Act, s. 5 and the 1975 Act, s. 140.

[52] For example, the Consequential Provisions Bill as originally drafted would have made all industrial injuries benefits taxable, which they had never been before; contrast the Bill as ordered to be printed on January 21, 1975, Sched. 2, para. 41 with the Consequential Provisions Act, Sched. 2, para. 39. Fortunately the error was discovered in time.

[53] During my time Mr. McQuitty, a Northern Ireland Queen's Counsel, was a member of IIAC, but apart from him none of the other bodies that I have mentioned affecting the Commissioners' field including NIAC contained a single lawyer.

[54] For one startling effect of the overlapping rules in relation to taxation see Decision C.S. 1/75 (not reported).

[55] See *Renton*, para. 18.29, p. 130.

[56] See n. 41, above.

[57] See the Acts of 1946, ss. 41 and 77 and 1965, ss. 88 and 108.

[58] See the 1973 Act, Sched. 12, para. 19 and the 1975 Act, Sched. 15, para. 18.

[59] See the N.I. (Guardian's Allowances) Amendment regs. 1962 [S.I. 1962 No. 1270], the F.A.N.I. Act 1961, s. 6, the 1965 Act, s. 29 and Decision C.G. 10/73 (not reported). The difference was that between temporary suspension (the Act) and permanent disentitlement (the regulations). The present regulations contain no provision for either disentitlement or suspension; see the Guardians Allowances regs. 1975 [S.I. 1975 No. 515], reg. 5.

[60] See the Acts of 1946, s. 77, and 1965, s. 108, the 1973 Act, s. 48 and Sched. 12 and the 1975 Act, ss. 138 and 139 and Sched. 15. The Notes on Clauses relating to the 1973 Act are curiously uninformative.

[61] See the I.I. Act 1946, s. 61. In cases of urgency there have always been powers to make national insurance provisional regs., but these were merely temporary; see the 1946 Act, s. 77 (4).

[62] See the 1973 Act, s. 48 and the 1975 Act, ss. 138 and 139 and Sched. 15.

[63] I have counted more than 15 such statutory instruments between S.I.s 1975 Nos. 458 and 566.

[64] See the 1975 Act, Sched. 15, para. 20.

[65] An alternative might be to have a separate Act for the many administrative provisions which are of no conceivable interest to the user. That however would not affect the principle.

[66] I believe that national insurance law, which is wholly statutory, is an exception to the general recommendation of *Renton* (paras. 14.6 to 14.10, pp. 86–87) to the contrary.

[67] This is not inconceivable. The home confinement grant was abolished.

[68] Including the provision contained in the 1973 Act, s. 99 (18) changing the name of the Ministry of Social Security Act 1966 as amended by the N.I. Act 1974, Sched. 4, para. 28 for certain purposes only.

[69] See S.I.s 1975 No. 1318 (C. 38), No. 1572 (C. 45), No. 1689 (C. 48) and No. 2079 (C. 58).

[70] For this, *Current Law* is invaluable.

Chapter Nine

EXAMPLES OF COMPLEXITY

SINCE I believe that it would be unhelpful and indeed cowardly for me to suggest that some things are wrong without venturing any opinion as to how they might be put right, I have devoted most of this chapter to an analysis of two enactments, one of industrial injuries law and the other of national insurance law, with a view to seeing whether either of them might be simplified.

The Special Hardship Allowance

The first subject is the increase of disablement benefit known as a special hardship allowance, now provided by section 60 of the 1975 Act, formerly by section 14 of the Industrial Injuries Acts 1946 and 1965. The origin of the increase was as follows. Under the Workmen's Compensation Acts the rate of compensation depended on the difference between the workman's earnings before the accident and what he was earning or able to earn in some suitable employment or business after it.[1] It inevitably followed that as soon as the workman had recovered from the accident sufficiently to resume his previous occupation he was no longer entitled to compensation, even though he still suffered some disability.

This rule was thought to be wrong. Accordingly the three Acts of 1946, 1965 and 1975 have always proceeded on a completely different basis. After the end of the injury benefit period the claimant may become entitled to disablement benefit,[2] frequently referred to as basic disablement benefit. The amount of it depends on the degree of disablement assessed by the medical authorities, the medical board or medical appeal tribunal.[3] This assessment takes no account of the claimant's occupation or his incapacity for it.[4] As however the Bill which became the Industrial Injuries Act 1946 was proceeding through Parliament it was realised that this system was going too far in the other direction. It did not distinguish at all between the cases of for example a labourer, who loses part of a finger but when it has healed is able to continue with his occupation, and a musician whom the same injury prevents from ever again following his occupation; or a miner on the coal face who is prevented by a back injury from resuming his work and a clerk with a similar injury who is not. Accordingly section 14 was inserted into the Bill which became the 1946 Act [5] though it had not been in the original Bill. Even after that Act had been enacted but before the appointed day for its operation very substantial amendments were made to section 14 by the National Insurance (Industrial Injuries) Act 1948 which received the Royal Assent on June 30, 1948, less than a week before the appointed day for the Industrial Injuries Act 1946. One amendment was to substitute a flexible sum for the fixed sum, which was a partial reversion to the Workmen's Compensation system.[6] It is evident therefore that at more stages than one there were second thoughts about section 14.

The purpose of section 14 stated in the broadest terms was to provide some compensation, in addition to basic disablement benefit, for the worker prevented by the accident from earning as much as he would have been able to earn but for it. I refer to this below as the broad purpose of the section.

The section,[7] like the later ones, laid down the two alternative conditions of title to the increase, always referred to as the permanent condition and the continuous condition. The first is contained in the words down to the end of paragraph (*b*) " suitable in his case; " and the second in the rest of subsection (1), which was added by the 1948 Act. A later subsection [8] shows how the amount of the increase is to be determined, not exceeding a statutory maximum, once a title to the increase has been established under subsection (1).

The phrase " special hardship allowance " has been criticised. A payment under the industrial injuries scheme takes the form of either a pension, an allowance or a gratuity. Disablement benefit takes the form of a pension or a gratuity, but never an allowance. A special hardship allowance takes the form always of a pension; never a gratuity or an allowance. The word allowance is therefore inappropriate. The origin of the phrase is to be found in the marginal note to section 14 of the Industrial Injuries Act 1946 which reads " Increase of disablement pension in cases of special hardship." [9] The wording of the marginal note to section 60 is similar though not quite identical. The description in Schedule IV, Part V, paragraph 6 follows the old form. The words " special hardship " are inappropriate, since it has never been suggested on behalf of the Department or the insurance officer that to prove a title to the benefit one must prove special hardship; indeed it is possible to think of cases where a person is financially better off drawing sickness benefit, disablement benefit and a special hardship allowance than when working.

The special hardship section may have been intended originally to fill a small gap. In practice it was found to play an extremely large part in the administration of the scheme, and still does so. The sections have been the subject of numerous decisions. The Jenkins Index, Volume 3, devotes some 90 pages or parts of pages to the subject. My own card index of Commissioners' decisions contains some six inches of cards. Numerous appeals have been considered by Tribunals of Commissioners.[10] A continuous stream of cases flows through the Commissioners' offices, the decisions in which very often cause great difficulty and in many cases dissatisfaction to the claimant, who is unable to understand the reasons for the statutory provisions. The difficulties of operating the section have been obvious to the Department and its predecessors for at least a quarter of a century, yet so far as I know neither the Industrial Injuries Advisory Council nor any other body outside the privacy of the Department has ever been invited to conduct a wide-ranging inquiry into its operation.

If it be accepted that the broad purpose of the section is as I have stated it, the first thing that will be noticed about section 60, like its predecessors, is that it takes a great many words and introduces a number of debatable concepts to arrive at the same destination. The reason may be historical. The deceptively simple words in section 9 (4) of the 1925 Act (as amended) had led to enormous difficulty and had resulted in numerous cases going to the Court of Appeal and the House of Lords.[11] The present legislation introduces a number of concepts, *e.g.* "the result of the relevant loss of faculty," the "regular occupation," "incapable of following" it, "employment of an equivalent standard," "suitable in his case," "subsidiary occupation" and "reasonable prospects of advancement." Each of these phrases has caused difficulty in administration. Possibly however the provision which needs the closest attention is that relating to "the beneficiary's probable standard of remuneration" in subsection (6). I will comment on these phrases one by one.

"As the result of the relevant loss of faculty." Special hardship claims are decided by the statutory authorities. It is, however, never their duty to decide whether an accident has resulted in a loss of faculty, nor what the loss of faculty consists of. The duty of deciding those questions is entrusted by statute to the medical board or medical appeal tribunal.[12] In the *Ward* case Lord Parker C.J. said: "It seems to me that the words of section 14 'the relevant loss of faculty' merely refer to the state found by the medical authorities to have existed after the accident, and at the time of their examination." His Lordship accepted a statement by a Commissioner that it is for the medical authorities alone to decide whether the relevant accident has caused a loss of faculty and in what the loss of faculty consists.[13] Lord Parker also said that a claimant cannot introduce a completely new loss of faculty on which to claim enhanced benefit but he can invoke a worsening in condition. In practice great difficulty has been experienced in applying these words. Where the injury is a simple physical one and the medical authorities' decision is comparatively recent there is little difficulty. Claims for a special hardship allowance, however, are often based on accidents which happened 10 or 20 years ago, where the medical authorities made a life assessment shortly after the accident on forms which do not require them to state what the relevant loss of faculty consists of. There may have been all sorts of subsequent developments. The relevant condition may have been recorded simply as a fracture, but osteoarthritis and perhaps some nervous condition may have developed which are alleged to result from the accident. Sometimes the medical board may have included a " functional overlay " as either being or not being a relevant condition. Doctors use this phrase to cover anything from blatant shamming to a perfectly genuine condition resulting from the suffering of continuous pain coupled with the failure of all efforts to provide relief or any hope of it. It may be extremely difficult, years after the accident, quite apart from supervening conditions obviously not due to it, to judge whether the claimant's present condition is to be treated as part of the relevant loss of faculty or resulting from it. Sometimes, *e.g.* in eye injury cases, he alleges that he is incapable of following his regular occupation due to fear of suffering a second similar accident; is he incapable as the result of the relevant loss of faculty? In many cases it is extremely difficult to decide as a matter of fact whether the condition at the relevant time and the accident are causally related. That difficulty is compounded when the question is not that one but whether the present condition is due to what the statutory authorities think that the medical board have decided constituted the relevant loss of faculty.

These difficulties suggest consideration of the question whether, if subsection (1) is to be retained in its present form, either " the relevant injury " or " the relevant accident " might be substituted for " the relevant loss of faculty." If it be objected that this might create conflicts between the different adjudicating authorities, two comments may be made. First, such conflicts already exist. The *Ward* case shows that even where the medical authorities have made a life assessment, based on the view that a relevant loss of faculty throughout the claimant's lifetime is to be expected, the statutory authorities can entertain evidence that there is now nothing wrong with the claimant resulting from the accident, which of course implies that there is now no relevant loss of faculty. Secondly, in view of the importance of special hardship claims, it might be worth considering whether the benefit should not be made a separate benefit of its own divorced from disablement benefit.

The claimant must next prove that the relevant loss of

faculty has resulted in inability to follow his regular occupation. This involves deciding what his regular occupation was at the date of the accident or the development of the prescribed disease. In the *Humphreys* case the Court of Appeal saw no difficulty about this problem. But in that case everyone agreed that the claimant's regular occupation had never been anything but that of a ripper; the question was whether that meant a ripper at a particular place or in a particular colliery or with some such limitation. There have been very many claims disputed on this question.[14] Questions arise whether a claimant has anything which can fairly be described as a regular occupation where he has only just started work, perhaps as a trainee, student or apprentice. At the other end of his career questions may arise whether he has abandoned his regular occupation merely temporarily or permanently or what should be regarded as his regular occupation where he has changed it. The regular occupation may be a combination of occupations, as in the case of the woman who did two different part-time jobs,[15] or a man who does shift work during the week with massive overtime in the same or different work for the same or different employers, perhaps over the weekend; here difficulties arise as to the meaning of a subsidiary occupation.[16] Sometimes the regular occupation has ceased to exist.

Here the question of prospects of advancement comes in. Section 60 of the 1975 Act contains two provisions, the first contained in the concluding three lines of subsection (2) beginning with the words "and in assessing the standard" and the second in subsection (3). They are not mutually exclusive, and in a proper case a claimant can seek to rely on both of them. The former provision only has always been in the Act. It was soon found to be a broken reed. It does not enable the statutory authorities to treat an occupation which the claimant would have been but was not following as the regular occupation, but it merely affects the calculation in relation to the actual occupation.[17]

The provision now in subsection (3) was introduced in 1961 [18] with a view to filling this gap. In my opinion even it does not go far enough. It requires the claimant to prove three things,[19] one of which relates not to himself but to others, namely " the persons in that occupation (or a class or description of them . . .)." It therefore may not help the wholly exceptional young person who would obviously have gone much further than any of his or her fellows. Many cases illustrate the difficulty of deciding what the regular occupation was when the employers and the claimant have called it all sorts of different things.[20]

It having been decided what the regular occupation was, the next question is whether as the result of the relevant loss of faculty a claimant is incapable of following it. This is often by no means a clear cut issue. As a result of an accident a man may be reduced to working more slowly or doing shorter hours; he may have been taken back partly on a charitable basis; he may be a member of a team, the other members of which are prepared to " carry " him. In practice the line between ability and inability to follow the regular occupation may be exceedingly difficult to draw. Moreover long before the *Mellors* case the question had arisen whether a man was capable of following his regular occupation even though he could not work such long hours or earn so much money.[21]

The next questions relate to employment of an equivalent standard and employment which is suitable in the claimant's case.

The former question gives rise to serious difficulties as to the burden of proof. On general principles it is for the claimant to show on balance of probabilities that he satisfies the conditions of title to the benefit which he is claiming. To prove however the negative, namely that there is no suitable employment of an equivalent standard which he could follow, places an enormous burden on him. In practice he says that he can think of nothing and the insurance officer after consulting the appropriate government departments suggests something which he might be able to do. If the claimant can persuade the statutory authorities that he could not do any of those occupations he probably succeeds on his claim. But the question arises whether suitable employment means actual employment available or hypothetical employment. Must it exist in the claimant's neighbourhood? If not, is he to be expected to move? If the claimant is a married woman, is she to be expected despite her marital obligations to move? [22] Where the length of the working hours in any suggested employment of an equivalent standard differs markedly from those of the regular occupation difficult questions may arise both under subsection (1) and as to the probable standard of remuneration under subsection (6). The decision of the Court of Appeal in the *Mellors* case above establishes what the law on this topic is, in effect reversing two of my earlier unreported decisions.[23] I am still however completely unconvinced that this is what the law ought to be. The propositions that, if a man by working double the hours in a new occupation can earn the same money, that employment is of an equivalent standard and the difference between his two standards of remuneration is nil, are to me totally unjust and unacceptable.

At many points both under subsection (1) and subsection (6) an extremely important problem has arisen, which may perhaps be described as the supervening unconnected incapacity problem. This can best be explained by an illustration. A man is employed on highly skilled, dangerous, demanding and very well paid work. He suffers an accident causing permanent injuries and will never be able to undertake that work again and will probably never be able to earn as much money elsewhere. Awards of a special hardship allowance are repeatedly made, and that is obviously right. As time goes on however a stage is reached when for reasons completely unconnected with the accident he would not have been able to continue in that employment, perhaps because he has reached retiring age or is now physically frail, or he has suffered some devastating illness such as a stroke (not resulting from the accident) which makes him permanently incapable of undertaking any employment at all. The question is whether it is right that he should continue to be paid a special hardship allowance for inability to do work which quite apart from the accident he would not be able to do. The House of Lords had to consider a very similar problem in connection with the words " he is earning or is able to earn in some suitable employment . . ." in section 9 of the Workmen's Compensation Act 1925. The same problem arose under the present legislation. What is the beneficiary's probable standard of remuneration in the employments which are suitable in his case and which he is likely to be capable of following (subsection (6)) where for extraneous reasons be cannot follow any employment or earn anything? This question came to a head in 1962, when a Tribunal of Commissioners presided over by myself gave Decision R(I) 14/62. As that decision shows, the view customarily taken by the Commissioners in earlier decisions had been that the section was to be read literally, and if the relevant loss of faculty caused a person to be incapable of following the occupations in question it did not matter that some other condition also made him incapable. In Decision C.I. 13/62 (not reported) one of the Commissioners Mr. Nelson took a different line. He accepted the insurance officer's submission that in a case of this type the claim failed. Other cases raising the same point arose, and I directed a hearing by a tribunal of Commissioners. In his written submission the insurance officer had supported Mr. Nelson's view. By the date of the hearing however he had turned completely round and submitted the opposite. The result was that the only arguments that the tribunal had, on behalf of the claimant and the insurance officer, supported the view that the claimant was entitled to succeed. It is perhaps therefore not surprising that we decided accordingly. It will be seen from paragraph 17 of the decision that we were told that about 25,000 people were continuing to receive a special hardship allowance over pensionable age, of whom about 10,000 were five years or more over that age.

In many circles today it is wholly unacceptable and indeed regarded as quite indecent to suggest that anyone who is receiving a benefit ought not to continue to be paid it. That is what I am suggesting now. I think that consideration ought to be given to the question whether this practice should be continued. It is not sufficient to say that little harm is done if many thousands of elderly people receive more money than logically they should. Such practices create injustice as between similar cases: if there are two men living next door to each other, each of whom is unable to work owing to old age, it seems to me completely wrong that one should draw a special hardship allowance for inability to do work which he would not be doing anyway, whereas the other should not.[24]

I have picked out some of the more prominent problems under the section which have given rise to argument. My own view is that the difficulties are and continue to be such that the time has come for a wide-ranging inquiry to see whether some simpler form of words more nearly approximating to what I have described as the broad purpose of the section might not operate more effectively and more justly than the present ones. Of course there is always a danger of jumping out of the frying pan into the fire, and in industrial injuries work we have had the most vivid experience of simplification in the words " arising out of and in the course of " the employment. It would however in my opinion be quite wrong to take the view that the experience of the last 25 years has resulted in an ironing out of all the difficulties. In the *Langley* case the court has accepted an interpretation of the words " regular occupation " where they are used in the Prescribed Diseases regulations [25] which is the opposite of a view commonly held for many years.

If the amount of the increase is to remain flexible and something like subsection (6) is to be retained, the complexity of the situation is apparent both from the decision and the judgments in the *Mellors* case itself and from Mr. Lazarus' subsequent explanation of it in Decision R(I) 1/72. Nevertheless an attempt should be made to see whether some more satisfactory form of words cannot be devised. Those cases demonstrate the serious administrative difficulties; but if they stand in the way of justice they must somehow be overcome.

If as a result of recommendations of the Royal Commission on Civil Liability and Compensation for Personal Injury section 60 or provisions based on it should be introduced into other branches of the law, that would be an additional argument for taking every possible step to ensure that the form of the provisions is as perfect as possible.

Retirement Pensions

I have chosen as my second subject for analysis the statutory provisions relating to retirement pensions. They are very important; the annual cost of such pensions is now of the order of £5,000 million.[26] I think that the subject illustrates some of the methods of legislation which are unhelpful to the user.

Retirement pensions were provided by the 1946 Act,[27] which laid down three sets of circumstances in which a person could be treated as having retired. These caused considerable problems owing to the vagueness of the language. Accordingly in 1960 a fourth alternative condition was provided[28]: if this condition, which related to the claimant's earnings, was satisfied, it was unnecessary to consider the others. This most satisfactory piece of legislation went far to resolve the problems, which is why there are far fewer decisions since 1960 on the original conditions.

The 1965 Act was merely consolidation,[29] but in 1970 pensions at a lower rate, corresponding to the present category C pensions, were introduced for people who had been over pensionable age on July 5, 1948,[30] and in 1971 retirement pensions corresponding to the present category D pensions were introduced for persons aged over 80,[31] and also increases for certain pensioners who had been in receipt of invalidity benefit.[32] The 1973 Act reproduced all these provisions with some alterations, and introduced the descriptions of them, categories A, B, C and D pensions.[33] As, however, the sections relating to these pensions were among those which were not to come into force until April 5, 1975, and were repealed on that day immediately after doing so, the names of the categories made no impact then.

The 1975 Act consolidated the 1973 Act in respect of these pensions.[34] Like the 1973 Act, it provides four categories of pensions at different rates described as category A, B, C and D retirement pensions. Category A is much the most important, relating as it does to persons of either sex relying on his or her own contributions.[35] Category B provides primarily for a wife who relies on her husband's contributions, though the Social

Security Pensions Act 1975 provides extensions of the Category B pensions, including such pensions for certain widowers. Both these types of pension are contributory. Category C and D pensions are non-contributory pensions and are intended for elderly people who do not qualify for category A or B pensions. The amounts payable for some of the pensions are flexible. There may be increases in respect of children or adult dependants [36] or where the pensioner has deferred retirement and continued to contribute after pensionable age,[37] or has been in receipt of invalidity allowance,[38] or has paid graduated contributions. In some cases it may be reduced owing to partial satisfaction of the contribution conditions,[39] or where the earnings of the pensioner have exceeded a certain amount during the period of five years after retirement.[40]

The relevant sections show that there are numerous groups of persons, who may be entitled to pensions at differing rates by satisfying different conditions relating to sex, age, retirement, and their or their spouses' contributions, earnings and other matters. Some of these considerations apply to some but not to all. This obviously poses problems as to the form in which the conditions for each group of persons should be described in the legislation. Of one thing I am sure. In the case of those for whom the conditions are simple they should be stated simply, and the user or his adviser should not have to read through sections irrelevant to him, to make sure that they are irrelevant. Since a man of 70 or more is entitled to a category A pension on two conditions only, namely that he has contributed enough and has claimed, the law should tell him that plainly and simply. At present he is told at the outset by section 27 (3) that he must have "retired from regular employment," which would probably lead him or his adviser to look into the question what "retired" and "regular employment" mean. He is next told by section 27 (4) that he must have "complied with the prescribed requirements as to the giving of notice of the date of his retirement," which would probably lead to a search to discover what those requirements are. They are in fact to be found not in the Widow's Benefit and Retirement Pensions regulations [41] but somewhat surprisingly in a Schedule to the Claims and Payments regulations.[42] It is only when the user reaches section 27 (5) that he is told that he is " deemed " to have retired on the expiration of five years after attaining pensionable age. This means in his case that the question whether he has retired from regular employment or not is totally irrelevant, and he has been wasting his time. And one effect of the words " Subject to the following subsection " in section 27 (4) is that he need not give notice of retirement. *But* (I assume, despite the absence from section 27 of the magic words " subject to the provisions of this Act " which were in the corresponding earlier sections) he must claim his pension,[43] and may lose some of it if he does not do so in time. Moreover he must read more, including the following sections, since any of them may, as in fact section 30 (1) does in the case of younger people, qualify sections 27 and 28.

If the user is a spinster her adviser needs to read the Acts [44] even more carefully to make sure that there are not other provisions relating to her as there are to married women and widows.

It seems to me that if one looks at these sections from the point of view of the user, they attack the problem from the wrong end, as did the Social Security Act 1973. The user's adviser presumably knows his client's sex and age. These facts will be their starting point. They should be helped to start from it; and they should not be required to read or search for statutory provisions which do not apply to them. But this is just what they are at present required to do. The situation of men over 70 and women over 65 in respect of category A pensions are totally different from those of people under those ages, yet their rights are dealt with in the same section as those peoples' and they are all included in the same category A.

I think that it would be possible to simplify matters by dividing people up into groups, and having a separate section or subsection which would deal exclusively and comprehensively with one group only, containing where necessary signposts to relevant provisions elsewhere. Pensioners can be divided into big groups by reference to sex and age only, though the groups would need to be divided further by reference to their matrimonial situations (if any).

A man's basic rights differ according to whether he was born before July 6, 1883,[45] or on or after that date but he is over 80,[46] or he is under 80 but over 70,[47] or under 70 but over 65.[48]

Similarly a woman's basic rights differ according to whether she was born before July 6, 1888,[49] or on or after that date but she is over 80,[50] or is under 80 but over 65,[51] or under 65 and over 60.[52] These are the four main age groups for whom pensions are available. The groups would need to be divided further according to whether the person is or has been married and may be entitled to rely on the contributions of a spouse, and whether his pension is to be increased or decreased for any reason or is affected by any circumstances.

I do not know whether any experiments have been done in the Department or elsewhere to try various ways of completely reframing the retirement pension provisions on these lines. This may be less simple now that contributory and non-contributory benefits have for the first time been put in separate Chapters of the Act. Presumably it would be necessary to start with a general section setting out the various groups by reference to age, sex and circumstances, for whom pensions are available, with signposts to the later individual sections. It might add some general provisions applicable to them all, *e.g.* that nobody is to be paid two pensions at the same time; and that (almost always) one must make a claim. Each following section would deal separately *and comprehensively* with one age group. It might of course do so by reference to others; for example, a spinster might be told that her rights except in the matter of age were identical with those of an unmarried man. But the essence of the matter is that it should be possible for the adviser of a person in a certain group to be sure that he knows all the conditions without having to look at the sections relating to other groups. If one is considering primarily the user's interests this would be worth while even if it resulted in a considerable lengthening of the statute. If at present there are eight relevant sections and he has to read them all, it would be advantageous to him if in future there were 16 but he had to read only two of them. Very exceptional or rare cases could be dealt with by regulations, to which the section would contain a clear signpost.[53]

I would hope that in conducting any such experiments consideration would be given to the following points. The title of the benefit is in itself misleading. Many persons under pensionable age have retired, but because they are under that age they are not entitled to a pension. Many others more than five years over pensionable age have not retired and have no intention of doing so, but they are entitled to a pension simply because of their ages. Retirement is therefore relevant only during the very limited period between pensionable age and five years older. In substance the pension is an old age pension. If the word " old " is regarded as a dirty word, some longer phrase which wraps it up such as a superannuation pension might be acceptable.[54] This point may increase in importance when section 30 (2) begins to have effect.

The use of the word " regular " qualifying the employment adds to the confusion. It is not the regularity of the employment that matters, but the circumstances at present set out in section 27 (3). Some women who work regularly, perhaps part-time, for a wage less than that referred to in section 30 and have no intention of doing anything else, attain the age of 60 but do not claim their pension because they are in regular employment and do not realise that they can. Pathetic cases of this type or of women working for quite high remuneration who become 65 and do not claim have come before the Commissioners. Probably there are others which do not come as far. Sometimes their claims have to be disallowed in part because of the absolute time limit for claiming.[56]

The following matters of detail may perhaps be noted. There is a technical though perhaps unimportant discrepancy between the definitions of " pensionable age " in section 27 (1) and Schedule 20 in that only one of them is subject to the words " unless the context otherwise requires." [57] I think that the word " may " in the first line of section 27 (3) ought to be " shall "; the section is conferring a right. Section 27 (3) (*b*) (i) contains three conditions which need to be considered separately. Experience shows that any condition which has not an identifying number wastes time—and time is money. It is easy to say that the condition in section 27 or in section 27 (3) or even in section 27 (3) (*b*) (i) is satisfied. It wastes far more words if the condition has no label and has to be described.[58] I do not know why the last three lines of subsection (3) of section 27 were inserted (first in the 1973 Act). Where a claimant by means of a misrepresentation, which may be fraudulent, persuades the statutory authorities that he is to be treated as having retired, the practice is to review the decision under what is now section 104, thus in effect cancelling his retirement and not merely disallowing the payment of benefit. It is to be hoped that the words do not interfere with this practice.

The age addition provided by section 40 (1) applies to contributory as well as non-contributory pensions, and being placed in the chapter relating to the latter might be overlooked in connection with the former.

I think that consideration might be given to making the Act refer not a person who *has* retired, which is an act coupled with an intention, but to a person who *is* retired which is a state or condition. Section 30 (3) enables regulations to provide that Part II shall have effect as if the person had not retired or become entitled to a pension. But people often misunderstand " deeming " provisions, and in particular they might not realise that such a person is " a person who has not previously retired " for the purpose of section 27 (5). The objective surely must be to avoid every conceivable source of misunderstanding. Section 27 (3) needs to be considered in connection with section 30 (3). If a man decides to retire for six months but after that to exercise his right to resume employment under regulations under section 30 (3) he in my opinion is or ought to be entitled to a retirement pension for the six months, and he ought not to be even tempted to make false statements about his intentions for the future.

Having discussed these two specific instances I will conclude this chapter with some miscellaneous suggestions of ways in which the interests of the user might be better considered.

The legal publishers and the editors of the Red Book and the Blue Book have over the years been introducing various devices designed to help the user, and the makers of statutes should be prepared to entertain any idea with an open mind. Loose-leaf editions of the statutes should be seriously considered.

Since in every branch of the law there are repeated expressions of failure to understand why the statutes are drafted as they are, there should in my opinion be far greater openness in the process of preparing and drafting them so that those concerned may form their own opinion on the wisdom of inserting this or excluding that or dealing with something in a particular way.

Provisions relating only to Northern Ireland, if included in a statute relating to Great Britain, should be clearly separate. The 1973 Act was in this respect most confusing to the user.

The short title of an Act should be short. The short title of what is now (for some purposes) the National Insurance Act 1970 must have wasted a lot of people's time before it was altered. Short titles should not be changed unless this is absolutely necessary, and if a change is made it should operate for all purposes. Even now the changes of the titles of the Supplementary Benefit Act 1966 and of the National Insurance Act 1970 apply only in Acts, instruments and documents.[59]

Under the present system small changes are slipped into consolidating Acts and regulations, and unless the user goes through all of them with a magnifying glass he will be unable to detect them or estimate their effects. In the past much use has been made in national insurance amending regulations of the device known in connection with statutes as a Keeling Schedule, which makes the nature of the changes clear. I think that much more use should be made of this device in both statutes and regulations. The Schedule might even be printed for use as an amendment of a loose-leaf version.

Some changes are obvious. They suggest that there may

be others that are not. Thus the words " following an occupation " are changed to " engaged in any employment " in a regulation which also contains the words " does no work," [60] a change which by reason of urgency was not considered by NIAC. In the 1975 Act itself I wonder why the cross-headings above sections 21 and 24 have been changed as they have, whereas that above section 14 has not.

A source of frequent inconvenience to the user is the use of general phrases such as " subject to the provisions of this Act " or " subject to the regulations." These make it necessary for him to search the whole Act and to discover what regulations there are. In my opinion the legislation should be specific: the maker knows what he has in mind, and he should say what it is.

A constant lookout should be kept for phrases which repeatedly occur, and some device should be invented to save repetition in respect of them. For example, if whenever there is an up-rating the rates of unemployment benefit go up on Monday, family allowances on Tuesday, pensions on Thursday, etc. (or whatever the days may be) a simple section providing that on all future up-ratings the rates should go up on those days next following the commencement of the Act unless otherwise provided would save a deal of repetition. Awards are made by the thousand for periods from date A to date B " (both dates included) "; a provision that in any document in this field both dates would be included unless the document said otherwise would also save trouble.

I have already expressed my pleasure at finding the glossary in the 1975 Act in Schedule 20. This admirable innovation should, however, I think be carried further: the qualifying words " unless the context otherwise requires " being in a section are liable to be overlooked and should appear at the beginning of the Schedule. Moreover on the next consolidation, when everyone has become accustomed to the number of that Schedule, it should remain unchanged. To facilitate this I think that we should entertain a new idea. We are accustomed to statutes which contain sections and Schedules. We should become used to ones containing sections, Schedules and a glossary, which would be cited by that name and would not be liable to have its Schedule number altered on amendment.

The amendment of a statute by inserting a section without stating where it is inserted is most inconvenient. The amendment of a statute by a regulation is worse because it is liable to be overlooked. When in the *Hurst* case the Divisional Court quashed the Commissioner's decision because he had not decided a diagnosis question, none of the judgments mentioned the regulation which governed the question whether he had any jurisdiction to do so.

Where a statute creates conditions which need to be considered separately they should be numbered separately. I have given some examples,[61] but this should be a general rule.

I think that a most important lesson to be learned from national insurance work is that wherever possible legislation should use concrete rather than abstract words, and words having a single, clear meaning. Since 1960 there have been far fewer Commissioners' decisions on the retirement conditions. The reason is that in that year Parliament added a new condition relating to earnings, which was far more specific than the existing vague expressions " occasionally," " to an inconsiderable extent " and " in circumstances not inconsistent with retirement." [62] The new provision, even though it contains the word " occasionally," is far simpler to administer. Vague words such as " normally " and " ordinarily " when used in the conditions of title to benefits have often caused difficulty.[63] And unfortunately some commonly used expressions are ambiguous or of doubtful meaning. If we say that on a certain day a man did not work, was not following an occupation and was not engaged in any employment, do we mean three different things and if so what is the difference? [64]

My last comment on legislation relates to the difficulty experienced by the public in obtaining it. Statutes, statutory instruments and other documents form part of the law of the land and are essential requisites of the user. They should be immediately available, by post if the user lives at a distance from a centre. If at any time they are not, or it appears likely that they will not be immediately available, the remedy should in my opinion be radical. Documents which constitute any part of the law of the land should be given absolute priority at every stage of production and distribution over all non-essential publications, however useful, so that the user can ascertain immediately and without difficulty the law which he and his client are required to obey.

Notes

[1] See the Workmen's Compensation Act 1925, s. 9.

[2] Under the 1975 Act, s. 57 (1965, s. 12).

[3] In accordance with the 1975 Act, s. 57 and Sched. 8; formerly the I.I. Act 1965, s. 12 and Sched. 4.

[4] See Sched. 8, para. 1 (*c*).

[5] *i.e.* the I.I. Act 1946.

[6] See Decision R(I) 7/69 (the *Mellors* case), para. 22.

[7] s. 14 in the amended form in which it came into force on July 5, 1948, is conveniently printed as a Schedule to the I.I. Act 1948.

[8] See the I.I. Acts 1946 (as amended in 1948), s. 14 (4), and 1965, s. 14 (6), and the 1975 Act, s. 60 (6).

[9] This phrase was repeated in the 1965 Act and also elsewhere when the rates of benefit were being altered and a description was necessary (*e.g.* the 1965 Act, Sched. 3).

[10] See the 1975 Act, s. 116.

[11] See Willis, *Workmen's Compensation* (37th ed.), p. 279 onwards.

[12] See the 1975 Act, s. 108 (1) (*a*), 1965, s. 37 (*a*), 1946, s. 36 (1) (*c*).

[13] In Mr. Owen George's Decision C.W.I. 1/64 reported as R(I) 2/65.

[14] See J 1359 to 1367.

[15] See Decision R(I) 33/58.

[16] See J 1361A to 1362.

[17] See J 1368A.

[18] By the F.A.N.I. Act 1961, s. 3.

[19] See Decisions R(I) 8/67 and R(I) 8/73.

[20] See *e.g.* Decision R(I) 6/75.

[21] See *e.g.* Decision C.I. 443/50 (reported).

[22] The difficulties are well illustrated by Decision R(I) 24/57.

[23] Decisions C.I. 18/68 and C.I. 29/68 (both unreported).

[24] To redress the balance, in some cases an adjustment of the basis of retirement pensions might be necessary.

[25] See the N.I. (I.I.) (P.D.) regs. 1959 [S.I. 1959 No. 467], reg. 37 now the S.S. (I.I.) (P.D.) regs. 1975 [S.I. 1975 No. 1537], reg. 38.

[26] At the April 1975 rates the amount exceeded £4,500 million (D.H.S.S. Annual Report 1974, p. 90), and in Nov. 1975 there was a substantial up-rating.

[27] See the 1946 Act, ss. 20 and 21.

[28] See the N.I. Act 1960, s. 3.

[29] See the 1965 Act, ss. 30–37, 40–42, 43A (a 1971 alteration) and 44–45.

[30] See the N.I. Act 1970, s. 1.

[31] See the N.I. Act 1971, s. 5.

[32] See the 1971 Act, s. 4, which inserted s. 43A into the 1965 Act.

[33] See the 1973 Act, ss. 23–28 and 35.

[34] See the 1975 Act, ss. 27–30, 33 and 34, 39–43 and 45–48, and the S.S. (Widow's Benefit and Retirement Pensions) regs. 1974 [S.I. 1974 No. 2059] (made in Dec. 1974 and therefore containing references to the 1973 Act and not the 1975 Act) as amended by the S.S. (Miscellaneous Amendments and Transitional Provisions) regs. 1975 [S.I. 1975 No. 566].

[35] See the S.S. Pensions Act 1975, ss. 8–12.

[36] See the 1975 Act, Pt. II, Chap. III.

[37] See s. 28 (4) and the S.S. Pensions Act 1975, s. 12 and Sched. 1.

[38] See the 1975 Act, s. 28 (7).

[39] See s. 33.

[40] See s. 30.

[41] See n. 34, above.

[42] See the S.S. (Claims and Payments) regs. 1975 [S.I. 1975 No. 560], Sched. 2, para. 4 (2).

[43] See the 1975 Act, s. 79, which contains some exceptions to the need for a claim.

[44] The 1975 Act and the S.S. Pensions Act 1975.

[45] See the 1975 Act, s. 39 (1) (*a*). I think this a better way of describing the situation than the statutory way. Many elderly people know or have a record of their date of birth, but may not know what pensionable age was and whether they were over it in 1948. As to the computation of age, see the 1946 Act, s. 78 (4), the 1965 Act, s. 114 (4), and the 1975 Act, Sched. 20, definition of age, and the Family Law Reform Act 1969, s. 9.

[46] See s. 39 (1) (*c*).

[47] See s. 27 (5).

[48] See ss. 27 and 28.

[49] See s. 39 (1) (*a*). See n. 45, above.

[50] See s. 39 (1) (*c*).

[51] See s. 27 (5).

[52] See ss. 27 and 28.

[53] It might even be helpful to construct either a chart like a chess-board, or alternatively two charts, one for each sex, with the age groups along the top and other circumstances relating to retirement, marriage, invalidity, earnings, etc., down the side; with, in the squares, signposts to the statutory provisions (including regulations) relevant to the combination of age and circumstances of anyone. Such a chart included as

a Schedule to the Act might be found to be a most valuable composite signpost.

[54] *Cf.* the title of Mr. Crossman's Bill. See p. 14, above.

[56] See the 1975 Act, s. 82 (2), and p. 32, above.

[57] See the 1975 Act, s. 168 (1).

[58] Other examples of this are contained in the description of the continuous condition in s. 60 (1), beginning with the words "or if as the result," and in s. 20 (4) in the words "but, after the lapse of such an interval."

[59] See p. 20, n. 28 and p. 100, n. 68.

[60] See the S.S. (U.S.I. Benefit) regs. 1975 [S.I. 1975 No. 564], reg. 7 (1) (*h*) and (*e*).

[61] See the N.I. (I.I.) (P.D.) regs. 1948 [S.I. 1948 No. 1371], Sched. II, as amended by the N.I. (I.I.) (P.D.) Amendment (No. 2) regs. 1949 [S.I. 1949 No. 1697].

[62] The 1975 Act, s. 27 (3).

[63] *e.g.* in the provisions referred to on p. 86, and in relation to seasonal workers (see [S.I. 1975 No. 564], above, reg. 19).

[64] See n. 60, above.

Chapter Ten

CONCLUSIONS

One of my main themes in these lectures is that, whilst the substantive law and the methods of changing the statute law could be improved, the three-tier adjudication structure is such a good one that it would be a most serious error to substitute for it something different. This however has on more than one occasion been proposed, and in this chapter I shall begin by making some comments on the contributions to the operation of the system made at the different levels, which I believe would not have been available under any different system.

I suppose that now it would be generally accepted that there ought to be power, as it is now clearly established that there is power in England, by which judicial or quasi-judicial decisions of tribunals can be set aside by the courts for error in law, the courts being the proper forum for declaring the law. I think that in our field there are special reasons why such intervention is desirable and indeed necessary. Apart from the general reasons that all specialist tribunals are liable to get into a groove and an occasional breath of fresh air from above may be highly healthy and salutary, there is a special reason relating to Commissioners particularly. Like the judges, Commissioners from time to time take different views on problems.[1] In the early days when there were five Commissioners a unanimous decision of a tribunal of Commissioners represented the view of the majority at least. More recently when there have been nine or 10 Commissioners this has not been so. In such a case it is specially desirable that the court should have power to settle the matter once for all by a judgment binding on all the Commissioners. I would hope that this power would not need to be exercised often, but it is essential that it should be there.

The influence which the courts can exert on the development of any area of law depends on how frequently decisions are challenged before the courts. If the parties hardly ever bring national insurance problems before the courts the main duty of interpreting the legislation must necessarily fall on others.

So far as I know a list of all the cases that have come before the courts in which a Commissioner's decision has been challenged has never been published, and therefore in the hope that it may be of some help to researchers I have included one, which I believe to be complete down to the end of 1975, at the beginning of the book containing these lectures. The number of cases since 1948 in which a decision of a Commissioner has been challenged in the courts in England is as follows: in the House of Lords three [2]; in the Court of Appeal 11 (including the three) [3]; in the Divisional Court fewer than 40 (including the 11).[4] The majority of applications have been unsuccessful. A Commissioner's decision has never been quashed in a national insurance as opposed to an industrial injury or attendance allowance case. No decision of a Commissioner under the Family Allowances Acts has ever been before any court.[5] During the same period I guess, without having made an accurate count, that the Commissioners gave some 60,000 decisions, of which a good many thousands contained some point of interest and were therefore numbered, and between 1,500 and 2,000 were reported.[6]

An important question arises here as to the position in Scotland. I believe that until 1975 no attempt had ever been made to challenge a Commissioner's decision in any court in Scotland. This suggests to me that it has been generally believed that this is not possible. Some learned authors state or suggest positively that it is not possible, but passages in Wraith and Hutchesson, which the authors state were contributed by Professor A. W. Bradley of Edinburgh University, suggest the contrary.[7] I understand that in 1975 proceedings were instituted in Scotland for the reduction of a Commissioner's decision,[8] and the result of these pending proceedings will obviously be of great interest. If it leaves any doubt but that there already exists in respect of Commissioners' decisions in Scotland a remedy comparable to that in England, presumably consideration will be given to the introduction of one by statute, since any difference in this respect between England and Scotland would seem to be a serious anomaly.[9]

As we have seen, there is a fundamental difference between the different types of appeal to a Commissioner. An appeal from a local tribunal is an appeal on fact as well as law. An appeal from a medical appeal tribunal or the Attendance Allowance Board is on law only. There are therefore completely different reasons why the present system should be retained in respect of both types of appeal and one must consider them separately. I am not sure that those who have suggested a two-tier system have attached sufficient weight to the differences.

Appeals from Local Tribunals

Any system of adjudication must take into account the scale of operations. In 1974 after some 16 million claims had been decided by insurance officers there were over 28,000 appeals to local tribunals and 1,850 further appeals from them to Commissioners.[10] The quality of appeals to the local tribunal varies almost infinitely. The answers to some, even if they are not actually frivolous, are clear and simple. Others are difficult and complex, though sometimes this is not apparent on the surface. The diversity of appeals calls for fairly refined sifting procedures to ensure that the difficult or complex cases receive the full treatment which they require, and not less important that the simple cases do not receive unnecessarily elaborate treatment, thereby clogging the whole machine to the detriment of other claimants. The present system provides a most efficient sifting at two levels, which achieves this object in a manner which I am sure a two-tier system could not do.

The first sifting process takes place when some of the claimants whose claims have been disallowed appeal to the local tribunal. But local tribunals sit in nearly 200 places throughout Great Britain, and it is too much to hope that in every case all the available evidence will be before the tribunal, all the correct legal considerations will be accurately stated by the claimant or in the insurance officer's submission to them, and their decision will be justified on the facts as well as being correct in law. In fact in 1974 out of 1,852 appeals to the Commissioner 572 resulted in a decision in the claimant's favour, which means, since the large majority were appeals by claimants, that the local tribunal's decision was reversed in a very substantial proportion of the cases where there was an appeal.[10] An appeal to a Commissioner provides a second and in my opinion essential further sifting process. Such an appeal is a rehearing in the full sense. If there is no oral hearing it is the Commissioner's duty to consider the case afresh on the facts as well as the law, taking into account not only all the evidence put before the local tribunal but also any further documentary evidence which may have been produced for the first time at the Commissioner level. If he holds an oral hearing every party has a statutory right to call evidence before him,[11] irrespective of whether it was called before.

Over the years a succession of able Chief Insurance Officers have built up in their office a high degree of expertise, which to a substantial extent is concentrated on appeals at Commissioner level and is of the greatest assistance to the Commissioners. If a two-tier system were substituted, this expertise would inevitably be spread over a far larger area with an inevitable reduction in its quality, instead of being concentrated where it is most needed.

The large majority of appeals to Commissioners as well as to local tribunals turn on questions of fact and degree, where different minds without any error in law may reach different conclusions. The existence of a right of appeal on fact to one of the comparatively small body of Commissioners, who are well placed to be familiar with each other's decisions and approaches to questions of fact, gives a good chance of preserving the delicate balance involved in deciding every case on its own merits but at the same time preserving uniformity of decision in similar cases, without which claimants would be dissatisfied and the law would be brought into disrepute.

The existing system has special advantages for claimants, and also from a financial point of view for their unions. Many claimants are unrepresented and are unable before the local tribunal to produce satisfactory evidence in support of their claims. It would be impracticable for the insurance officers in tens of thousands of cases coming before tribunals to anticipate this and obtain the missing evidence if that were possible. On a further appeal to the Commissioner however where the number of cases is far smaller sometimes the evidence is available for the first time at that level, in many cases as a result of the initiative of the insurance officer then concerned with it. For the unions also the advantages are great. If the local tribunal's findings of fact were final it would be necessary in cases where medical evidence was relevant for them to go to expense in obtaining the best medical evidence in every case. Under the existing system they can, and some of them in fact do perfectly legitimately, take their chance before the local tribunal with such evidence as they have and concentrate the expenditure on the most expert evidence in the small number of cases which reach a Commissioner, thereby avoiding either a denial of justice or a greater expenditure of their funds.

Of course with an unlimited right of appeal to a Commissioner without leave in all cases since *Franks* a certain number of frivolous appeals come before them, but they are not the ones which occupy the time of either the insurance officers or the Commissioners. They concentrate their experience mainly on the difficult cases.

I have heard it suggested that if a two-tier structure were substituted a President of a strengthened local tribunal system would be able in effect to do the whole of the sifting process himself, by picking out difficult or important cases and arranging for them to be dealt with in some special manner, perhaps by a full-time as opposed to a part-time chairman. In my opinion this would be completely impossible. If anyone had asked me when I was Chief Commissioner to pick out the most difficult and complicated cases even from the far smaller number of appeals in the Commissioners' London office alone I could not have done so, even by devoting an immense amount of time to the process. Difficulty and complexity are not always evident, and they sometimes emerge at the hearing itself for the first time.

If the Commissioners became full-time chairmen of a "strengthened" local tribunal system, I have no doubt that this would be bound to dissipate their expertise also and greatly lower the quality of their work.

There would be other consequences of the substitution of a two-tier for a three-tier system. Numerous decisions of Commissioners show that since 1948, and therefore long before the creation of the Council on Tribunals, the Commissioners have been exerting a powerful influence on the manner in which local tribunal proceedings are conducted. Where on an appeal to him the Commissioner detects any irregularity, breach of the regulations or unfairness at the local tribunal level he has not hesitated to say so in his decision, thereby bringing the matter to the notice of the members of the tribunal, and where the case is reported or numbered to others.[12] In fact during the 10 years preceding the Franks report the Commissioners had already been exercising much the same influence as is now exercised by the Council on Tribunals, but with the very important difference that a Commissioner can not only criticise any mishandling of the case; he can also if appropriate reverse the decision. The Council cannot do that. Since the creation of the Council the Commissioners have continued to exercise influence in this way with, I believe, the full approval of the Council, thereby in effect supporting and supplementing the Council's work. Having dealt with very many appeals the Commissioners are familiar with every aspect of local tribunal proceedings and are therefore able to achieve this very effectively. In a two-tier system no one tribunal nor even its chairman would have any authority to reverse or criticise the conduct of another tribunal, with the result that irregularities would go unchecked, except in the few cases that went to the courts.

A further disadvantage of a two-tier system concerns reporting. From personal experience I can say that the selection of decisions for report is an extremely difficult and time-consuming one, even when one is dealing with only the decisions of nine or 10 Commissioners. To select a reasonable number of decisions for report out of the whole number of those given by a local tribunal system would in my opinion be completely impracticable; and I cannot think how the system of numbering decisions not reported but still containing some point of interest could survive.

The value of the present system is illustrated on the occasions, fortunately comparatively rare, when experience shows that an earlier decision requires reconsideration. No one has ever sought to challenge the view always taken by the Commissioners that the doctrine of "*stare decisis*" does not apply to them. This makes it comparatively simple for a tribunal of Commissioners or even an individual Commissioner to refuse to follow an earlier decision.[13] Where however a principle of law has been laid down by a court it may be much more difficult to get it reversed. It may be necessary to go to an even higher court, and, as the dates in the *Dowling*, *Hudson* and *Jones* cases show, this may take a very long time; and in the end it may be unsuccessful. With a two-tier system no local tribunal would have any authority over any other, and the effect might well be to put local tribunals into much the same position as the medical appeal tribunals before the 1959 Act,[14] when the inconsistencies between their decisions on questions of law caused that Act to be passed.

I have no doubt that the three-tier system should be retained, and I respectfully echo what the Chairman of the Council on Tribunals wrote to the Lord Chancellor on February 27, 1970: "There is great value therefore in the present right of appeal from the Local Tribunal to the National Insurance Commissioner, which is much cheaper, quicker and more suitable than appeal to the High Court, and by which uniform standards can much more rapidly be established." [15] If in answer to these arguments it is suggested, as in fact it has been, that in place of the present remedy in the High Court on the ground of error of law there should be substituted a two-tier system with an appeal on fact as well as law to the High Court, in my opinion this would not provide anything approaching a satisfactory solution. It would be an attempt to merge two completely different systems. Claimants would almost certainly lose the advantages of informality, speed, etc. to which the Council on Tribunals have referred. Many questions would need to be considered. Would the rules of evidence apply as they do in courts but not before tribunals? Would the claimant and the insurance officer retain their right on the appeal to call witnesses who had not been called below? Would the claimant retain his present advantage of having his costs paid within limits and not being liable to any award of costs against him on an appeal? These are only some of the difficulties. My belief is that the effect of such a change would simply be that many claimants who now appeal to the Commissioner owing to the ease of doing so, some of whom succeed, would simply not appeal to a court and there would thereby be a denial of justice. I think too that similar difficulties would have resulted if the claimant in the *Punton* case had succeeded in persuading the Court to make a declaration inconsistent with the Commissioner's decision.[15a]

I shall not attempt any full analysis of the numerous decisions by Commissioners over the years on appeals from local tribunals which have affected the development and interpretation of the law. I hope however that it will not be thought invidious if I select one decision illustrating strikingly the result that can follow from an appeal to a Commissioner, which I believe would not have been achieved under any other system. I refer to Mr. Lazarus' Decision R(I) 12/68. The claim was for industrial injury benefit, the allegation being that the claimant as a result of lifting a heavy wardrobe at work suffered a myocardial infarction. A series of medical decisions [16] had shown how difficult it is for such a case to succeed unless the effort involved was quite exceptional. The only medical evidence before the Commissioner was that of a senior medical officer of the Department; it was unfavourable to the claimant's case. In view of some evidence given earlier in the same year in a case the subject of a numbered decision,[17] Mr. Lazarus doubted the correctness of the view recorded in the medical decisions. He therefore called for further evidence, which was supplied by the insurance officer, together with references to medical works, which Mr. Lazarus considered with a medical assessor who sat with him at the hearing. When the views of the assessor were communicated to the insurance officer, the Department took what Mr. Lazarus described as the admirably constructive course of inviting the Royal College of Physicians to nominate two eminent cardiologists to be asked to comment on the evidence and the assessor's views and to answer certain questions which, with their answers, are printed as an appendix to the decision. The answers of one of the cardiologists were favourable to the claimant's case and those of the other were not unfavourable. On receipt of the answers the insurance officer made a further submission supporting the claimant's appeal, which was allowed. I find it impossible to believe that this result could have happened under a two-tier system. It resulted from the Commissioner's knowing of the evidence in the earlier (unreported) case, the presence with him of an assessor who to some extent disagreed with the views of the senior medical officer and that in the medical decisions, and the obtaining of the opinions of the two cardiologists. It seems immensely improbable that all these factors would have been present in combination under any other system. There was an interesting subsequent development. In January 1974 Dr. Carmichael [18] gave a talk to the Medico-Legal Society entitled "Medical Aspects of the Industrial Injuries Act: Some Illustrative Case Studies," [19] in which he discussed Decision R(I) 12/68. We therefore have the two points of view, that of the Commissioner from his decision and that of the doctors from this talk. The admissibility of Medical Decisions as evidence is established by the *Moore* case, but I think that one lesson to be learnt from Decision R(I) 12/68 is that they should be used with the utmost caution, lest an obsolete medical doctrine continue to be applied because neither the Commissioners nor the department doctors feel justified in taking the first step to question it.

Appeals from Medical Appeal Tribunals

I turn now to the first "extension": appeals from medical appeal tribunals, with which I shall deal separately although appeals from the Attendance Allowance Board are similar in principle, except that the Board has no power to grant leave to appeal.

I referred earlier to the circumstances in which an appeal to the Commissioner was introduced in 1959 after it had become well known that medical appeal tribunal decisions were amenable to certiorari and various divergencies had appeared in decisions coming from different districts, all of which made it probable that a considerable number of them would be challenged in the High Court.[20] The introduction of a right of appeal to the Commissioner seems to have had the desired effect. During the years after 1959 the Commissioners decided a very large number of applications and appeals, and I have been unable to find any certiorari proceedings either from a medical appeal tribunal direct or from the Commissioner on appeal from such a tribunal between the *Hubble* case in 1958 and the *Dowling* case in 1965. This suggests that the Commissioners were making a real contribution to solving the legal problems. Moreover it was the Commissioners rather than the Council on Tribunals who were, when necessary, impressing on medical appeal tribunals the necessity for adhering to the rules of natural justice.[21] I cannot remember any Annual Report of the Council on Tribunals in which this topic was commented on in relation to medical appeal tribunals (or later the Attendance Allowance Board). The Commissioners were doing it as early as 1961. Moreover it soon became the practice that since most claimants were completely unable to recognise an error in point of law, if an arguable one was noticed by the Secretary of State's representative [22] or by the Commissioner they would draw attention to it and if appropriate the Commissioner would give leave to appeal so that the point could be discussed on the appeal. The possible consequences are illustrated by the *Hubble* case. There were there two issues, and the one with which we are concerned did not go beyond the Divisional Court. The claimant had appealed to a medical appeal tribunal alleging that an assessment at five per cent., made by a medical board, was insufficient. The tribunal heard the case (in 1957 before the 1959 Act), and without any warning they not merely did not increase the assessment but they set it aside altogether. After failing to get that decision reviewed, the claimant took proceedings in the High Court for an order of certiorari. The Divisional Court in 1958 dismissed the application, explaining that the tribunal had had power to do what they did. In the *Howarth* case in 1968 Lord Denning M.R. delivering the judgment of the court, with which the other Lords Justices agreed, drew attention to the *Hubble* case and said that he would be inclined to say that in that case, as in the *Howarth* case, it would be contrary to natural justice for a new point to be taken against a man without his being given an opportunity of dealing with it; but he added that as (in the *Howarth* case) this point had not been pursued before the Commissioner or the Divisional Court it was not right for the Court of Appeal to rest their decision upon it. In 1961 however, seven years before, a tribunal of Commissioners had decided this very point. In one case it was held that if a decision of a medical appeal tribunal was arrived at after procedures which offended against the rules of natural justice, that made the decision erroneous in point of law and liable to be set aside by the Commissioner [23]; and the same tribunal had immediately applied this in a " surprise " case,[24] where the facts were in principle similar to those in the *Hubble* and *Howarth* cases, and had allowed the claimant's appeal, which the Secretary of State's representative had supported. Lord Denning's statement in 1968 was therefore a confirmation of the line which we had taken six years before and had repeatedly followed in later cases, in some of which the point was taken in favour of a claimant by either the Secretary of State or the Commissioner, though this does not always appear in the decision. A practice of the Commissioners which has operated greatly to the advantage of claimants concerns the duty of medical appeal tribunals to give reasons for their decisions.[25] Such a tribunal is a fluctuating body not in permanent session and the practice of the Commissioners where reasons are insufficient has always been not to ask for further ones but simply to set aside the decision, with the result that the claimant's case is reconsidered by the tribunal, almost always differently constituted.

The extent of this side of the Commissioners' work is shown by the following figures. In 1974 the Commissioners considered 261 applications for leave to appeal from medical appeal tribunals, granted leave in 46 cases (in addition to eight cases where leave had been granted by the tribunal itself), heard 63 appeals, of which 61 were by claimants, and allowed 39 of them.[26] If a two-tier system were substituted it would be necessary to decide where these applications and appeals and also those from the Attendance Allowance Board should go. If they went to the High Court that would be putting the clock back to before the 1959 Act, with all the disadvantages of the previous system. I have never heard it suggested that they should go to local tribunals, which I think would for many reasons be completely inappropriate, even if the latter were strengthened, especially as the existing chairmen of local tribunals have had little experience of dealing with medical appeal tribunal cases, since they do not come to the Commissioner by the ordinary statutory authority ladder. One of the virtues of the present system is that those concerned get the best of both worlds in the form of a quick, cheap appeal from a medical appeal tribunal on a point of law to a Commissioner, who has dealt with a considerable number of such cases, with the right if the Commissioner's decision is considered unsatisfactory to apply to the High Court to quash it. Since 1959 there have been only 11 such cases in the High Court, in seven of which the Commissioner's decision was quashed.[27]

There have not yet been any applications or appeals from medical appeal tribunals in mobility allowance cases.[28]

Appeals from the Attendance Allowance Board

I now turn to the other "extension," appeals to a Commissioner from the Attendance Allowance Board or its delegate.

An attendance allowance, which was introduced first by the National Insurance Act 1970,[29] is a national insurance benefit completely unrelated to industrial disablement benefit, but it is frequently erroneously referred to as a constant attendance allowance, which is and since 1948 has been an increase of industrial disablement benefit payable where the beneficiary requires constant attendance.[30] A *constant* attendance allowance differs from nearly all other industrial injuries benefits or increases of benefit in that exceptionally the duty of deciding whether the increase should be granted or renewed has always been entrusted to the Secretary of State (formerly the Minister) and not to the statutory authorities for decision.[31]

The introduction of the new attendance allowance in 1970 must have posed for the legislature and its advisers very serious procedural problems. Entitlement to the benefit depends on amongst other things the answer to certain medical questions relating to a requirement of attention or supervision by day or night.[32] One problem was who should decide whether these medical conditions were satisfied. It was obvious that many claimants would be incapable of attending any form of hearing and some would be completely helpless. It may well be therefore that the existing procedure for deciding title to the constant attendance allowance influenced the choice of the procedure for deciding these questions,[33] which is briefly as follows.[34] The Department provide a form for claiming and supplying information. The claimant is asked to read a leaflet which tells him that once the claim has been made there is nothing more for him to do. A medical report from a doctor is obtained by the Department on a form containing questions drafted by them. On the strength of this report and any other information supplied by the claimant the Board, or usually in practice their delegate, give a favourable or unfavourable decision on the medical questions. The insurance officer on the strength of that and in the light of his decision on any non-medical questions either allows or disallows the claim. A decision on the medical questions can be reviewed. If this happens a report is obtained from another doctor, again on a departmental form, and a review decision is then given by the Board or its delegate. There is no express statutory provision enabling the Board to hold any form of hearing, and so far as I am aware one has never at any stage been held by the Board or its delegate, though it has been suggested on behalf of the Department that one could be.[35] Neither the claimant nor anyone representing him ever sees the person who decides the medical questions nor knows who he is until the decision is received. There is no appeal from such a review decision on the facts. There has however, always been a right of appeal to a Commissioner with leave on law only against a review decision.[36]

Many of the considerations which I have discussed in relation to appeals from medical appeal tribunals apply in this field equally, and I need not repeat them. Here also the Commissioners made an immediate and substantial impact. In the very first numbered decision reported as Decision R(A) 1/72 the Commissioner Mr. Temple laid down in unmistakable terms that in giving a review decision the Board must comply with the rules of natural justice, the nature of which he explained by reference to High Court decisions; and he made it clear that the Commissioners were going to adopt the same strict attitude about giving reasons that we had adopted in medical appeal tribunal appeals. In a case in 1973 [37] which received considerable publicity, after allowing the appeal on the ground of insufficient reasons I added some comments on natural justice. The case bore similarities to those of *Hubble* and *Howarth* already referred to. There was a considerable body of evidence tending to support the view that the medical conditions were satisfied, but the Board without giving any intimation of their intention to do so decided that they were not. I commented unfavourably on the procedure. As a result of this decision forms of letter were introduced, one of which is sent in such a case to the claimant, telling him of the opinion which the Board had provisionally formed and thereby giving him an opportunity of submitting further evidence. Another decision [38] related to a " kidney machine " case. It was as a direct result of some comments made in that case that the Board shortly afterwards began to hold that in such cases the medical condition was satisfied. I think that it can fairly be said that in this field also the Commissioners, though limited to deciding questions of law, have been able to exert a powerful influence on permissible approaches by the Board to mixed questions of law and fact.

It may of course be argued that the courts could and would have done the same thing better. Such an objection however is based on the assumption that the courts would have been given the opportunity of doing so. I think that the figures make this improbable. 1973 was the year when the initial surge of appeals came before the Commissioners: the figures are therefore probably maximum ones. In 1973 there were 435 applications for leave to appeal to a Commissioner; leave was granted in 248 cases; 287 appeals were considered, of which no fewer than 267 out of the 287 were allowed, nearly all of them being appeals by claimants.[39] The 1974 figures were lower but substantial: 94 applications; leave granted in 20; appeals decided 32; appeals allowed 25 out of the 32. When one takes into account the various advantages to the claimant of an appeal to a Commissioner compared with proceedings in the High Court, I do not believe that anything like one-tenth of the successful appeals would have reached the court at all. In fact no claimant has yet challenged an attendance allowance decision of a Commissioner in the High Court.

Nevertheless in this field also there can be no doubt that recourse to the courts on a question of law is essential. The medical conditions have always included the words "day" and "night." These words can have different meanings in different contexts. Conflicting decisions were given by Commissioners as to the construction of the medical conditions in respect of the word "night."[40] The Secretary of State accordingly took the question to the High Court, whose judgment settled the matter.[41]

The view which I am putting forward that the extended-three-tier structure is admirably suited to its purpose has received powerful support over the years, as the following examples show. It accords with the Franks Committee's description of "the ideal appeal structure."[42] In *Law Reform Now* Professor Griffith suggested the setting up of a copy of it in another area of law.[43] I have already mentioned the opinion of the Council on Tribunals in February 1970,[44] and it can be inferred that the Council later, after full investigation, did not approve a suggestion emanating from the Department that the three-tier system might be replaced by a two-tier one. The history of that matter is briefly as follows. In December 1970 it was announced in Parliament that the whole of the national insurance arrangements were under examination.[45] A working party was set up in the Department, but it was only at a very late stage in November 1971 that I learned that consideration was now being given to amalgamating local tribunals and Commissioners into one tier under a presidential system. There followed a number of discussions. Various papers were written. The Council on Tribunals requested the view of the Commissioners, which we gave, and in March 1972 three of us attended by invitation a meeting of a consultative group which the Council had set up to consider the suggestion. At that meeting the matter was fully discussed. The Council's Report for 1971–72 contained only an interim reference to the matter.[46] There was however no further reference to it in the Council Report for 1972–73 or in any later Report, from which it can be assumed that the Council did not favour the suggested change.

Professor Kathleen Bell (a member of the Council) and Professor Harry Calvert evidently favour the three-tier system, since each of them has recommended a further extension of it.[47] Finally, in his Upjohn Lecture on January 9, 1976, Lord Justice Scarman paid a remarkable tribute to it. After drawing a clear distinction between the adjudication systems for supplementary benefits and national insurance benefits respectively, he continued as follows:

> " . . . an admirable legal system culminating in the National Insurance Commissioners has been devised to make certain that recipients get their rights. Whatever criticisms one is tempted to make of national insurance, absence of legal control is not one. The system recognises in practice that the insured has rights, and that disputes must be determined judicially according to law. Difficult questions arise, particularly in regard to trade disputes, self-induced unemployment, marriage, and children: and they are being determined by National Insurance Local Tribunals, and on appeal by National Insurance Commissioners. A

substantial case law exists and is being further developed. There is emerging a healthy jurisprudence based upon a theory of rights obtained by contributions duly paid. Only one feature is presently lacking—legal aid at public expense; and that will surely come."

Later in the lecture Lord Justice Scarman recommended for supplementary benefit adjudication not that the administrative element in the scheme should be discarded but that the safeguard of a tribunal system effective to ensure legal control over issues of entitlement and disentitlement should be added to it. He said:

> "I would recommend that a system be devised on the model of the National Insurance Commissioners. If this were done it would not be necessary to provide any resort to the ordinary courts beyond that which already exists. The High Court would retain its supervisory power exercisable by prerogative order. Without such a system, I fear that we shall not achieve what Lord Denning said in *Moore's* case was required of the law, namely that 'there should be uniformity of decision.' Indeed, *Moore's* case illustrates how the supervisory power of the High Court is no substitute for a properly co-ordinated tribunal system."

Those words were spoken after the bulk of my lectures had been written. They strikingly confirm a number of opinions that I have been expressing.

It must not however be thought from what I have said that I should be opposed to any change. Expansion of the system, as happened when family allowance cases were brought within it, or further extensions may well deserve consideration. I see no objection to a proposal which the Council on Tribunals favoured in 1970 that the decision of Secretary of State's questions should be entrusted to local tribunals and Commissioners [48]; nor to further extensions such as a right of appeal in supplementary benefit cases to a Commissioner, as recommended by Professor Kathleen Bell after full investigation.[49] Professor Calvert has very recently suggested amalgamating supplementary benefit tribunals and national insurance local tribunals in a single system with an appeal to a Commissioner in all types of case.[50] This proposal goes further than Professor Bell's in that there would be an appeal to a Commissioner on fact as well as law. But it would preserve the three-tier system; it may therefore be compared with one of the 1959 changes when the decision of Family Allowance claims was entrusted to the statutory authorities.

The Report of the Royal Commission on Civil Liability and Compensation for Personal Injury has not (at the date when I am writing this in February 1976) been published. Whether or not the Report recommends the introduction of a "no fault" scheme, I can see no insuperable difficulty about adapting the industrial injuries scheme as administered by the statutory authorities to cover all or part of the area now covered by common law claims, so as to give injured persons the advantages of it such as indexed periodical payments in place of or in addition to lump sum awards.

I hold no strong view on the question whether the present remedy by way of a prerogative order (in practice certiorari) might be replaced by a right of appeal from a Commissioner on law only, with leave, either direct to the Court of Appeal or to the Divisional Court.

There have however been other proposals, comments and criticisms of the system with which I wholly disagree; I discuss them briefly. It is not uncommon for them to be expressed in general terms, so that sometimes it is not clear who is being referred to, either because of the ambiguity of the expression "social security" or because the critic may be unaware that a Commissioner is a tribunal.

One suggestion put forward in a Fabian Tract published in December 1973 was that social security tribunals should be replaced by courts on the County Court level, with an appeal on law and a limited appeal on fact to a newly constituted Social Division of the Court of Appeal.[51] I am wholly opposed to these proposals. I think that the substitution of a court would result in the most serious changes for the worse in respect of evidence, informality, speed, costs and other matters;

many of the advantages of the present system would disappear. The change would be rather like a reversion to the old Workmen's Compensation system, which was abolished because it was unsatisfactory. Of course if the change were merely a change of name and the features of a tribunal were retained, the result might be merely that those who at present attend tribunals but dislike lawyers and are frightened of courts would stay away, which would not be much of an improvement of the system. I am equally opposed to the suggestion of an appeal on fact, whether limited or not, to the Supreme Court. It would be inapplicable to decisions by Commissioners on appeal from a Medical Appeal Tribunal or the Attendance Allowance Board, where the appeal to the Commissioner is on law only and not fact and nobody has suggested a change in that. I believe that experience in the United States of America has shown that it is very difficult to create or maintain any limit on appeals on fact. The *Anisminic* case has shown that error in law within the boundaries of jurisdiction may have much the same legal consequences as going outside the boundary. In fact for many years the courts have corrected such errors, for example in the *Ward* and *Cable* cases, where the questions raised related solely to the construction of the legislation. Moreover Lord Diplock has written:

> " if the material before the reviewing Court discloses that the decision under review is one which the Court would have reversed if it had come up on appeal from a lower Court of law, legal reasoning is never at a loss to find a way of reversing it despite its classification as administrative."[52]

From time to time it is suggested that social security tribunals are not independent in that they are biased in favour of the Department. Owing to the vagueness and ambiguity of the charge it goes unanswered, and some people may believe it to be true. So far as it relates to national insurance tribunals I am certain that it is completely untrue. The Commissioners are and always have been completely independent, and I doubt whether suggestions to the contrary are aimed at them. As to chairmen of medical appeals tribunals and local tribunals I have no doubt that they are independent too. They cannot be appointed or removed without the approval of the Lord Chancellor or the Lord President.[53] The medical appeal tribunal chairmen are distinguished lawyers, some of whom have held high judicial office overseas. Local tribunal chairmen are mainly local solicitors, with a few academic lawyers and barristers, none of whom as a class has the reputation of excessive affection for government departments. For 16 years I spent much time studying not only the decisions of tribunals but also the complaints and arguments based on them in appeals before me. I attended five of the first six conferences of local tribunal chairmen in various regions.[54] I therefore had many opportunities for assessing whether they are independent. I can only say that I am confident that they are.

Finally, it is sometimes suggested that the social security system is a threat to the rule of law or to the law itself. I believe this view to be incorrect and based on two fallacies. The first is to regard social security law as if it were not part of the law of the land. Of course legislation is affected by government policy. But once a statute has been enacted and rules made under it in statutory instruments they are just as much part of the law as is the common law. Even if they are new branches growing on the legal tree they are part of the tree. Benefits are not awarded or refused by the statutory authorities in accordance with administrative policy or discretion. During the whole time that I was a Commissioner there was no single occasion when any government department or the Lord Chancellor's office or the Council on Tribunals attempted to influence the decision of a Commissioner by any direction or intimation of policy or any other means. The statutory authorities decide claims in the light of the legislation as interpreted in any decisions that may have been given by the courts or Commissioners. Indeed the main purpose of reporting decisions is to provide local tribunals and insurance officers with the necessary guidance as to how the law has been laid down—publicly.[55] The Commissioners are always seeking to interpret the legislation and administer the law on precisely the same lines as the courts and, though sometimes we have been unsuccessful, in none of the cases which have gone to the courts has it ever been suggested that we were trying to do otherwise. Secondly, it is fallacious to confuse the lawyers with the law. The difference between them is frequently blurred; for example by the title of the *Law List*: that publication does not list law; it lists lawyers. Social security law may well be, and I think is, a challenge to lawyers, and an opportunity for them, so long as the legal profession remains an honourable profession whose first object is to provide a service to the public. Whether in other circumstances it could become a threat to them is a question which I hope will never arise. But saying either of those things is completely different from saying that it is a threat to the law.

May I conclude by briefly summarising some of the most important thoughts that I would like to leave with you. Each of the National Insurance Commissioners is a tribunal administering justice in accordance with rules contained in legislation and available to everyone. I believe that some of the rules of substantive law could be expressed more clearly without changing their purposes, but that the extended-three-tier-plus adjudication structure serves its purpose admirably. I have no doubt that the law administered by the statutory authorities is an important branch of the law, and that neither social security nor the law governing it constitutes any challenge or threat to the law or the courts. Its administration is complementary to the work of the courts. If the judges are to be regarded as the regular soldiers in the front line defending the rule of law against those who are attacking it, the tribunals are a second line of defence, like territorials, backing up the regulars and supplementing their work. Social security law does present a challenge and an opportunity to the legal profession, but that is a different matter.

The future

As to the future, I hope that the extended-three-tier structure will not be reduced to a two-tier one; but that every effort will be made to achieve a simplification of the substantive law;

that an advisory body covering the whole field will be created as giving us the best chance of achieving that simplification; and that more members of the legal profession will play a part in this branch of the law. I state my hopes in that order—intentionally. The ideal would be legislation so clear and simple, and according so closely with the ideas of justice held by Miss Hamlyn's "Common People," that there would be little need for the services of lawyers to interpret it. But that is a long term aim, and for parts of its administration there will always be a need for lawyers. There are encouraging signs that interest in this branch of the law is increasing both in universities and elsewhere, and if anything in these lectures is helpful to anyone wishing to study it or help with its administration, then they will have served a purpose.

Notes

[1] *e.g.* in the *Ward* and *Rowlandson* cases. As to the latter see n. 40. below.

[2] The *Dowling*, *Hudson* and *Jones* cases.

[3] The *Punton*, *Moore*, *Humphreys*, *Culverwell*, *Cable*, *Howarth*, *Viscusi* and *Mellors* cases.

[4] These figures exclude cases where the application was abandoned and the court did not give a judgment.

[5] For court proceedings in respect of F.A. Referees' decisions see *Kirkwood or Fraser* v. *M.N.I.*, 1947 S.C. 594, and *Hill* v. *M.P.N.I.* [1955] 1 W.L.R. 899, and of a local tribunal's decision see *R.* v. *Hoxton Local Tribunal, ex p. Sinnott, The Times,* March 12, 1976.

[6] As to numbered and reported decisions see pp. 75–77, above. For the figures of reported decisions see J Vol. 3, App. 3.

[7] See *Franks*, Chap. 10 especially para. 110, and Wraith and Hutchesson, *Administrative Tribunals* (1973), p. 9 and Chap. 1, p. 30.

[8] The *Watts* case.

[9] An English case from the north of England posed a curious problem. It was to be heard orally by a Commissioner in Edinburgh because that was the nearest and most convenient forum. It became clear from the papers that the claimant's union wished to take the case further to the High Court if they lost. It was therefore arranged that the case should be heard in London, in view of the doubts about the situation in Scotland. For a wide-ranging discussion of the power of the courts in Scotland see the Scottish Law Commission Memorandum No. 14 *Remedies in Administrative Law* including the views expressed therein at p. 52.

[10] All the figures in this chapter are taken from the D.H.S.S. Annual Report 1974, Chap. 10.

[11] See the S.S. (D.C.Q.) regs. 1975 [S.I. 1975 No. 558], reg. 3 (3).

[12] A number of decisions in which Commissioners have pointed out to local tribunals how hearings should be conducted are collected in J Vol. 2, pp. 714 onwards.

[13] See for example Decisions R(G) 3/62 and R(I) 4/67. Before Decision R(I) 4/67 the problem of short breaks for necessary refreshment had for many years been a festering sore giving rise to numerous appeals. That decision, given in a case where the insurance officer had supported the claimant's appeal, settled the matter. Decision R(U) 7/68 shows how on occasion, though very rarely, a tribunal of Commissioners may decline to follow a rule of very long standing accepted by a previous tribunal of Commissioners and the Umpire before them, if satisfied that it is erroneous. See further, p. 74, as to the meaning of "stare decisis."

[14] The F.A.N.I. Act 1959. See pp. 11–12, above.

[15] See the Annual Report of the Council on Tribunals for 1969–70, App. B, p. 32.

[15a] See Preface.

[16] See para. 10 of Decision R(I) 12/68. As to Medical Decisions see p. 74, above.

[17] The subject of Decision C.I. 39/67 (not reported).

[18] Dr. J. A. G. Carmichael, F.R.C.P. was at the time of the hearing a principal medical officer of the department, but by the date of his talk he was Chief Medical Adviser (Social Security) to it.

[19] The talk is recorded in the *Medico-Legal Journal* (1974), Vol. 42, Pt. 2, p. 44.

[20] See pp. 11–12, above.

[21] See *e.g.* Decisions R(I) 28/61 and 29/61.

[22] Appeals from a local tribunal to the Commissioner have always been handled by an insurance officer but appeals from the medical appeal tribunal or the Attendance Allowance Board by the Secretary of State's representative.

[23] Decision R(I) 28/61.

[24] Decision R(I) 29/61.

[25] See the S.S. (D.C.Q.) regs. 1975 [S.I. 1975 No. 558], reg. 23.

[26] D.H.S.S. Annual Report 1974, para. 10.8, p. 102.

[27] Calculated as stated in n. 4, above.

[28] As at the date when this was written in Jan. 1976.

[29] Then called the N.I. (Old persons' and widows' pensions and attendance allowances) Act 1970, but renamed the N.I. Act 1970 for certain purposes by the N.I. Act 1972, s. 8 (4) (since amended). Provision had been made for it in Mr. Crossman's 1969–70 Bill, which was never enacted.

[30] See the I.I. Acts 1946, s. 15 and 1965, s. 15; now the 1975 Act, s. 61.

[31] See p. 18, n. 8.

[32] See the N.I. Act 1970, s. 4 (2) (single rate) replaced by the N.I. Act 1972, s. 2 (1) (higher and lower rates), now the 1975 Act, s. 35 (1).

[33] In a letter of Feb. 27, 1970, the Chairman of the Council on Tribunals in a letter to the Lord Chancellor wrote that the Council's latest discussions with the Department suggested that the (Attendance Allowance) Board would in reality review claims in an administrative rather than in a judicial manner; see the Annual Report of the Council on Tribunals for 1969–70, App. B, p. 32.

[34] See Decision R(A) 1/73, paras. 3 and 31. There are no statutory regulations governing the procedure of the Attendance Allowance Board.

[35] See Decision R(A) 1/73, para. 31.

[36] See the N.I. (A.A.) regs. 1971 [S.I. 1971 No. 621], Pt. VII and the S.S. (A.A.) regs. 1975 [S.I. 1975 No. 496], Pt. VI.

[37] The subject of Decision R(A) 1/73.

[38] Decision R(A) 2/74.

[39] See the D.H.S.S. Annual Report 1973, p. 87.

[40] See Decisions R(A) 4/74 and C.A. 9/72, and C.A. 1/74 (both unreported).

[41] See the *Rowlandson* case, quashing Decision R(A) 4/74.

[42] See *Franks*, Chap. 10, paras. 105 and 171.

[43] See *Law Reform Now* (1963), ed. Gardiner and Martin, p. 55.

[44] See p. 129, above.

[45] See Hansard, Dec. 15, 1970, Vol. 808, col. 1312, and the Report of the Council on Tribunals for 1970–71, p. 5, para. 19, referring to their report for 1969–70, p. 11, para. 47.

[46] See the Council's Report for 1971–72, p. 5, para. 20.

[47] See nn. 48 and 50, below.

[48] See p. 40, n. 26.

[49] See Kathleen Bell, *Research Study on Supplementary Benefit Appeal Tribunals. Review of Main Findings: Conclusions: Recommendations* (1975, H.M. Stationery Office). *Cf.* Hodge, *Really: Yet Another Tribunal*, L.A.G. Bulletin, Nov. 1975, p. 287.

[50] See Harry Calvert's Chap. 14, " Appeal Structures of the Future " in *Justice, Discretion and Poverty* (1975–76), ed. Adler and Bradley.

[51] See Fabian Tract No. 427, " Tribunals: a social court? " by Julian Fulbrook, Rosalind Brooke, and Peter Archer, published by the Society of Labour Lawyers. The Tract was the subject of a most unfavourable review by Professor Harry Street in the L.A.G. Bulletin, June 1974, pp. 128–129.

[52] See Schwartz and Wade, *Legal Control of Government* (1972), at p. xiii, foreword.

[53] See the Tribunals and Inquiries Act 1971, ss. 7 and 8 and Sched. 1, paras. 18 and 40A, the latter of which was inserted by the Consequential Provisions Act 1975, Sched. 2, para. 46.

[54] At Edinburgh, Leeds, London, Cardiff and Liverpool.

[55] *Cf. Franks*, para. 102.

INDEX